Marketing Essentials

Marketing Essentials

Jim Blythe

AMSTERDAM • BOSTON • HEIDELBERG • LONDON • NEW YORK • OXFORD
PARIS • SAN DIEGO • SAN FRANCISCO • SINGAPORE • SYDNEY • TOKYO
Butterworth-Heinemann is an imprint of Elsevier

Butterworth-Heinemann is an imprint of Elsevier
The Boulevard, Langford Lane, Kidlington, Oxford, OX5 1GB, UK
30 Corporate Drive, Suite 400, Burlington, MA 01803, USA

First edition 2008

British Library Cataloguing in Publication Data
A catalogue record for this book is available from the British Library

Library of Congress Cataloging-in-Publication Data
A catalog record for this book is available from the Library of Congress

ISBN: 978-0-08-096624-3

For information on all Butterworth-Heinemann
visit our website at elsevierdirect.com

Printed and bound in Great Britain
10 11 12   10 9 8 7 6 5 4 3 2 1

Contents

CHAPTER 1

The Nature and Scope of Marketing

Learning objectives

After working through this module and reading around the subject, you should be able to:

- Explain the evolution of marketing orientation.
- Describe the contribution of marketing as a means of creating customer value and competitive advantage.
- Describe the factors which contribute to a marketing-oriented approach to run the organisation.
- Be aware of the difficulties which might be encountered in developing a marketing orientation within the firm.
- Explain the cross-functional role of marketing.
- Explain the impact of marketing activities on consumers, society and the environment: marketing ethics.
- Be aware of the role of relationship marketing.

WHAT IS A MARKETER?

Marketers tend to think differently from other people in the organisation. This is because they are much more concerned with people, and especially people outside the organisation, than are (say) the finance manager or the production manager. Marketers tend to be risk-takers: they are more prepared to try something new, because this is usually the only way to establish a competitive advantage over other firms – following a standard, tried-and-tested approach means simply copying what other people have done, which will not generate any advantage. For this reason, marketers tend to be creative and innovative.

Marketers often think of themselves as having common sense: after all, if the company does not look after its customers, the customers will soon find someone who will and will spend their money elsewhere. To a marketer, this seems obvious, yet to many managers from other disciplines, it does not – they see the marketers as someone who is paid to go out and find customers for products which the company already supplies.

If the finance managers of two companies in the same industry were exchanged, they would almost certainly be able to carry on with their jobs without pause: the same would be true of company lawyers or administrators. If the marketers were exchanged, though, they would be completely lost in each others' firms because each marketer should be following a completely different programme of new product development, promotion, pricing and so forth. This is because each marketer seeks to differentiate his or her company from all the others in the market, as a way of reducing (or at least circumventing) the competition.

THE EVOLUTION OF MARKETING ORIENTATION

Marketing is a relatively young discipline and is thought to have evolved from previous business paradigms as follows:

1. Production orientation. In this paradigm, the key to success in business is to produce as cheaply as possible and keep prices low. This paradigm was typical in the 19th century, when mechanised production could out-compete hand production in cost terms. The basis of production orientation is that people will buy anything as long as it is cheap enough. The drawback, of course, is that consumers are expected to accept a standardised product which is unlikely to meet their needs exactly: only a very few products are acceptable on a one-size-fits-all basis. Many firms still operate this way, but people have come to expect (and can afford) more customised products, and global production runs mean that economies of scale can still be generated. The drawback from a manufacturing viewpoint is that the company is competing on price, which invariably cuts profit margins: there is always someone somewhere in the world who is able to produce more cheaply or is desperate enough (or naïve enough) to sell below the costs of production.

2. Product orientation. In order to compete effectively, the product needs to have features which appeal to individual consumers. In a product-oriented firm, the products are designed to incorporate a large number of features in order to meet the needs of a large number of consumers. Such products can become extremely complex, since people's needs vary considerably, even for basic, everyday products such as biscuits and cleaning materials. Unfortunately, the cost of a 'state of the art, all the bells and whistles' product becomes too high for most people, and of course consumers do not want to pay for features which they are unlikely ever to use.

3. Sales orientation. As mass production developed to the point where there was an over-supply of goods, firms supposedly switched to a sales orientation. Sales-oriented firms believe that people will only buy if they are subjected to a high-pressure sales pitch: the assumption is that people do not want to buy things and will only do so if persuaded. Furthermore, sales orientation assumes that people will not mind being persuaded and will be happy for the salesperson to call again: from the producer's viewpoint, success is thought to come through using aggressive promotional techniques. In effect, sales orientation aims to change customers in order to meet the needs of the organisation. The major problem from a producer's viewpoint is

that salespeople are an expensive item, so much so that it is almost always cheaper simply to produce things that people want to buy. Sales orientation has little or nothing to do with the practice of selling, of course: high-pressure techniques simply result in cancelled orders once the sales rep has left.

4. Market orientation. Here the firm looks at what the market (i.e. consumers) actually needs and acts accordingly. For the market-oriented firm, the customer's needs and wants are at the centre of everything the firm seeks to achieve, and the aim of the firm is to fit the firm to the customers rather than try to fit the customers to the firm. One key element in market orientation is that consumers can be grouped according to their needs, so that quite large subsections (or segments) of the market can be identified and targeted accordingly. Different products can be offered to each group, which enables the firm to compete by differentiation rather than competing on price: provided the cost of making changes is less than the additional premium people are prepared to pay for a more 'customised' product, the firm will make a greater profit and will also shut out competition, at least for a while. Market orientation means that customer needs become the driving force throughout the supplying organisation: a truly market-oriented firm will use customer need as the 'touchstone' for setting policy, for resolving differences between different departments within the firm and for considering competitive responses. Customer orientation is the degree to which the company understands its customers: the better understanding the firm has of their needs, the better it will be able to make more attractive offers, for which the firm can charge a premium price. Competitor orientation is the degree to which the firm understands the other offers in the marketplace: other firms may offer radically different solutions to the customer's needs, but each firm needs to consider whether the alternatives represent better value from the customer's viewpoint. Identifying who the competition is can be a major problem in itself – bus companies compete not only with each other, but also with trains, cars, bicycles, aeroplanes and even, in some cases, with the Internet. Some people have managed to cut out commuting by working from home, but most bus companies would not recognise this as competition.

A more recent addition to the evolution of marketing debate is the concept of societal marketing. This is the view that marketers should take some responsibility for the welfare of society as a whole and for the long-term sustainability of their activities. This need not necessarily conflict with meeting the everyday needs of consumers, but it does add another dimension of decision-making. For example, Kotler et al. (2001) have developed a classification of products according to their immediate satisfaction potential and their long-term benefits or disadvantages. Products which are highly satisfying and also have high long-term benefits are classified as desirable products: a natural fruit juice which is high in vitamins and also tastes good would fit this category. Products which are not immediately satisfying but which have high long-term benefits (such as a household smoke alarm) are categorised as salutary products. Products which are bad for people in the long run, but are satisfying in the short term (such as alcohol or confectionery) are called pleasing products. Finally, products which are neither good for people nor satisfying are called deficient products: for example, slimming products which do not work or toys which have no educational value and are boring to play with. In theory, firms should aim to produce desirable products, but consumers often choose pleasing products instead, for example, eating unhealthy foods when they feel unhappy (Garg et al. 2006).

There is considerable academic debate about whether the marketing concept actually evolved in a linear manner. In other words, there may not have been the kind of orderly move from production orientation to market orientation that is implied by the model: however, there is little doubt that the different orientations do exist and companies do operate under the various paradigms to this day. In fact, the company you work for may well not be market oriented – you may want to consider the implications of this.

The orientations themselves can still be seen in daily life: some companies are sales-orientated, employing high-pressure salespeople to persuade people to buy. This might be typical of a home improvements company, because there is unlikely to be much repeat business: selling someone a new kitchen or a fitted bedroom is usually a one-off process, as is selling time-share properties or even cars. Production orientation exists in many Far Eastern countries, where, for example, T-shirts or baseball caps are produced in their millions, with only a few sizes being available. Product orientation is staging something of a renaissance with the advent of iPhones: people are moving towards the idea of one piece of equipment that functions as a GPS set, as a camera, as Internet access, as a word processor, as a music system and so forth. Many teenagers no longer wear watches, because their telephones will tell them the time.

MARKETING IN PRACTICE:
The Kirby Cleaner

This example shows how a company with a product orientation (and, to some extent, a sales orientation) can still be successful. However, we might ask ourselves whether the company would do better if it were customer oriented.

Jim Kirby produced his first cleaning system in 1906, using water to separate the dirt from carpets and soft furnishings. This product was not a great success, since it left everything wet and also required the owner to clean out dirty water from the machine. In 1907, Kirby produced the first of his vacuum cleaners, using air to force the dirt into a cloth bag, but it was in 1925 that he launched the first multi-attachment vacuum cleaner.

Right from the start Kirby used door-to-door salespeople to sell the vacuum cleaners. As time went on, the product became steadily more sophisticated, with special attachments for cleaning bedding, curtains, linoleum, sofas and chairs and indeed almost anything else in the house which needed a clean now and then. The Kirby Cleaner could even be configured either as a cylinder model or as an upright model, as these competing designs came into the market in the 1930s and 1940s. The latest version has a multi-speed motor allowing it to be used to buff floors, and it has a carpet shampooing function, a special pet-hair removing attachment, and even a headlight for cleaning under furniture.

In fact, the Kirby Cleaner solves all the cleaning problems any normal householder will ever encounter, and does it extraordinarily well. So how come it is not the biggest selling vacuum cleaner in the world?

First is the price. With all the attachments, it costs over £1200 – which is quite a lot of money for a vacuum cleaner. Second, it is complex to use, and most people soon get tired of fitting each different attachment – once the novelty has worn off, most people only use it for basic carpet cleaning. Third, some people do not like the sales pitch. The salesperson comes to the customer's house and vacuums various items (the bed being one – people are amazed at how much dirt comes out of their mattresses). Almost everybody finds this embarrassing, and many find it intrusive – but equally, many find it hard then not to buy the cleaner, when this appears to be an admission that they do not mind living in a dirty house and sleeping in a dirty bed.

The Kirby Cleaner provides us with a prime example of a product-oriented company and, to a large extent, a sales-oriented company. The product has all the features anyone could want, but of course most people will only want two or three of the features and will not want to pay £1200-plus for a lot of features they do not need and will never use. Since the product would be unlikely to sell in a normal electrical retail outlet, the company has resorted to home demonstrations and powerful sales pitches – to be fair, the cleaner's amazing cleaning power would not be evident without a demonstration, but the cost of sending sales people out to people's homes is obviously extremely high.

The company has been selling vacuum cleaners for over 90 years now and operates in 70 countries with millions of satisfied customers. They must be doing something right! The question remains: Does Kirby's approach to the competitive world of vacuum cleaner marketing remain effective in the 21st century?

Equally, many companies are not truly marketing oriented. Some only say that they are customer-centred, without actually having a very clear idea of their customers' needs: it is very common for managers to guess what their customers might need rather than find out through market research or by careful analysis of the market.

THE CONTRIBUTION OF MARKETING

Marketing operates on the basis of adding value for customers. Marketers always begin by considering customer needs, whatever the business problem: customers are at the centre of everything they do, whether developing a new product which will make life easier and more convenient for consumers or designing an advertising campaign that will entertain, inform and catch the attention of the target audience. Creating customer value means that people are more likely to be prepared to give them their money, and they are more likely to return to them when they need something new: it has been said that marketing is about selling products that do not come back to customers that do.

Customer value is a key concept in marketing because it gives importance to the idea that we should always be looking for ways to improve the customers' experience of dealing with us and with our products. Customer value can be increased by adding something that our competitors do not have – although care should be taken not to slide into product orientation by providing everything that any customer could possibly want. The value should only be added if either it costs us nothing to do it or the cost will add less to the price we sell for than the value gained by the customer. If this were not the case, the customer would not see the product as continuing to offer value for money and would simply shop elsewhere. Customer value should not be confused with customer lifetime value, which is the value of the customer to the firm and is a key concept in relationship marketing.

Of course, marketers are not looking after the customer out of altruism. Meeting customer need effectively is the easiest way of creating an exchange (usually financial) and therefore is the most effective way for the firm to meet its own objectives. Marketing is not, therefore, about persuasion or fooling people: it is about providing useful, desirable products and services at a price that people regard as reasonable (or good) value for money.

If we are better at recruiting and retaining customers than our competitors, it seems likely that we will be able to compete more effectively in general. Customer retention has become even more important in recent years, and this has led to the development of relationship marketing, in which long-term relationships are established with customers so that an income stream is generated rather than a one-off transaction. There is a great deal more about relationship marketing throughout the course, since it is seen as the logical next stage in customer centrality.

CASE STUDY: Tesco

This case study shows how customer orientation works in practice. Tesco supermarkets are to be seen in every town throughout the United Kingdom and have become hugely successful through considering the needs of customers first. In less than 100 years, the company has gone from a market stall to a giant retailer, meeting the needs of widely differing groups of customers, despite strong competition from other supermarket chains.

In 1919, a young Londoner called Jack Cohen used his First World War Army gratuity to start a business selling groceries from a market stall in the East End of London. His fledgling business went well enough for him to start his own tea company, in partnership with a man by the name of T.E. Stockwell. Stockwell's initials plus the first part of Cohen's name provided Tesco with its brand name.

In 1929, Cohen opened his first grocery shop in Burnt Oak, Edgware. His motto was always 'Pile it high, sell it cheap' and during the depression-hit 1930s this proved to be a winning formula. During the 1930s, Cohen opened many more stores, but it was not until after the Second World War that supermarket methods came to Britain. Tesco's first self-service store was opened in 1948, and their first true supermarket was opened in 1956, in a converted cinema in Maldon. Because staff costs are much lower in supermarkets, and because Cohen was able to buy in bulk, prices should have been much lower at Tesco stores than in other stores, but until 1964 manufacturers were allowed by law to fix the retail prices of their goods. In other words, all retailers had to sell at the same price, so price competition was impossible. Tesco attacked this problem in two ways—first, the company gave out trading stamps which loyal customers could collect and redeem against gifts of household goods, and second, Jack Cohen was active in lobbying Parliament for a change in the law. In 1964, the Resale Price Maintenance law was repealed and Cohen was able to pursue a vigorous price-cutting approach to business (although trading stamps continued until 1977).

During the 1960s the United Kingdom experienced a rapid rise in prosperity. More people owned cars, more people owned freezers (and so were able to bulk-buy their food) and credit cards were just beginning to be used. In 1967, Tesco introduced the concept of the edge-of-town superstore when the company opened a 90,000-square-foot store at Westbury in Wiltshire. This store was intended to be used by car drivers—ample parking, large trolleys for bulk-buying and a much greater range of goods in the store meant that car owners could shop much more easily. The edge-of-town location meant lower costs for the store, which could be passed on to customers. This policy proved hugely successful, so through the 1970s Tesco gradually closed down its town-centre stores (with their high overheads) and concentrated on out-of-town superstores. In 1974, the company began selling petrol at discounted prices, again encouraging motorists to come to the store. By 1991 Tesco was Britain's biggest independent petrol retailer.

In the 1990s Tesco returned to the city centre by opening Tesco Metro stores, smaller supermarkets with a smaller range of goods and smaller pack sizes, designed to meet the needs of the local community and inner city dwellers. In 1997, the first Tesco's Extra superstore was opened, offering a range of non-food goods, household appliances and clothing, as well as the traditional groceries available in all Tesco's stores. Altogether, Tesco operates six different store formats: Tesco Extra, Tesco Superstore (standard-sized supermarkets), Tesco Metro, Tesco Express (neighbourhood convenience stores, mainly stocking high-value convenience products) and One Stop, which is a hangover from the company's purchase of T&S Stores in 2002. This is the only format without Tesco in the title and will probably be incorporated into the Tesco Express format eventually.

In 1995, Tesco was the first retailer to offer a loyalty card. Customers present the card at the checkout, and the Tesco central computer records their purchases. Every 3 months the customer receives a mailing containing vouchers which are redeemable at Tesco stores for groceries or other products; customers also receive special discount vouchers for specific products. Other retailers followed suit, offering their own loyalty cards, but by then Tesco had already seized a substantial market share. A spin-off from the loyalty scheme was that Tesco now had very detailed information about each customer's purchasing behaviour—how often they shop, where they live and what products they buy. This has proved invaluable for future planning and for fine-tuning the service to meet customer needs more effectively and was reported as having been used to thwart Wal-Mart's entry into the UK supermarket business through its Asda subsidiary.

Tesco's customer focus has moved ahead of Jack Cohen's 'Pile it high, sell it cheap' price competition focus. Being cheap is no longer enough—because every other supermarket chain operates on the same basis. Tesco found that most people object to queuing in supermarkets—so they introduced the 'one in front' system. If the queue is such that there is more than one person in front of the customer, the store opens more tills until either all the tills are open or the queue has subsided. The system is monitored centrally—every 15 minutes the tills freeze and can only be released by the cashier entering the number of people in the queue. The figure is fed through to Tesco's main computer, and if there are more than two people in the queues for more than 5% of the times the number is entered, the store manager is asked for an explanation.

Tesco has three own-brand ranges: the 'Value' range, which consists of cheap basic products; the 'Tesco' range, which aims to compete head-on with mainstream brands; and the 'Tesco's Finest' range of upmarket, luxurious products. Each brand meets the needs of a different group of Tesco customers. These now represent about half of all Tesco sales. The company also offers a range of organic products and is now Britain's biggest retailer of organic products. In 2000 the company launched Tesco.com, its online retailing system, which is the biggest online grocery outlet in the world. The online system owes its success to the fact that it is based in the stores themselves, not in a central warehouse, so that staff have local knowledge and the delivery routes are shorter.

Tesco's advertising uses the strapline 'Every little helps' and usually consists of products photographed against a white background, with a voice-over explaining the latest offers. The voice-overs use various well-known British actors such as Jane Horrocks, Martin Clunes, Terry Wogan and Dawn French: in 2007, the company's Christmas campaign featured The Spice Girls. Tesco also takes the lead in new product development: in 2009, they announced that they had developed a new type of tomato which is less juicy, so that it does not make sandwiches soggy. The company has also extended the brand hugely, offering mobile phones (using the O2 network), financial services such as insurance and savings accounts and even loans and credit cards. On the PR front, Tesco sponsors The Tesco Cup, a football competition for young players throughout the United Kingdom, and continues to offer its Computers for Schools programme, in which shoppers can collect vouchers to give to local schools which can redeem them against computer equipment. This scheme has been hugely successful: it encourages a sense that Tesco cares about the local community, while giving customers the chance to be generous towards local schools. It encourages people to shop in the stores rather than elsewhere, of course, but it also has a less obvious spin-off: Tesco has created a generation of computer literate people who feel positive towards the company and would make good employees.

Tesco's customer orientation has certainly paid off. It is now the United Kingdom's leading supermarket chain with 17% of the market. It operates in 10 countries overseas and is the market leader in 6 of those: 45% of the company's retail space is outside the United Kingdom. The company now offers personal finance products (insurance, credit cards, loans) at the checkout and has many other innovations on the way – customer champions, innovative buying policies and so forth.

All of which is a very far cry from a market stall in the East End.

Questions

1. Having low costs coupled with high prices must have made Tesco very profitable in the 1950s and the early 1960s. Why would Jack Cohen have lobbied for the abolition of Resale Price Maintenance?

2. Presumably Tesco's various customer-focused innovations cost money. Why not simply cut prices even further?

3. Why have three separate own-brand labels?

4. What is the difference between the trading-stamp system and the loyalty-card system? What advantages do loyalty cards have for customers and for Tesco's?

5. Why stock a range of organic products as well as ordinary products?

ASPECTS OF THE MARKET-ORIENTED APPROACH

Marketing can be viewed in several different ways, according to its role and status within the organisation:

1. **As a process of managing exchange.** Many academics define marketing as the process of managing exchange, and from a practitioner viewpoint this is not at all a bad definition. Managing the exchange process means that each party will be better off than they were before: if this were not the case, trade would be impossible. One of the problems with the definition is that many exchanges would not, by most observers, be regarded as marketing: an offer to help a friend with his car maintenance in exchange for help with the garden is certainly an exchange, but most people would not regard it as marketing. The key issues with this definition are that it is the marketers who manage the exchange process, and the exchange itself makes both parties better off – therefore, marketers seek to make it as easy as possible for the exchanges to happen (e.g. by ensuring that the products are readily available or that financing packages are available). The more exchanges that happen, the better off will the company be.

2. **As a driving philosophy of the business.** This means that the firm devotes all its efforts to meet customer needs, and every decision at every level of the firm is taken with the customer in mind. Note that customers and consumers might not be the same people – the purchase may be a gift or it may be a family purchase where one person makes the buying decision, with the needs of the other family members in mind. In such cases, the customer (the person doing the buying) has needs even if the product is for someone else, for example, a need for a convenient location from where to buy the product or perhaps for sales assistance in choosing the most appropriate product. Customers may be professional buyers buying on behalf of a company, in which case they will have very specific needs in terms of career aspirations and so forth. Astute marketers consider the needs of everyone involved in buying and consuming their products. If marketing is the driving philosophy, it acts as a coordinating force within the firm: everyone in the company will be aiming for the same end goal, customer satisfaction, and the marketers will have the role of ensuring that everyone is aware of customer needs and their own role in meeting those needs.

3. **As a managerial function.** If marketing is viewed as a managerial function only, the company will take marketing decisions on the basis that they will move the company nearer to its objectives, which may be shareholder value, growth, survival, profit or any one of many possible objectives. This moves marketing to a somewhat lower

position than it would otherwise occupy if it were regarded as the driving philosophy of the business, but marketers will still occupy a position of importance with regard to the other business functions of production, finance and personnel management. This role is probably typical of many successful companies – it is certainly possible to be successful without being entirely customer-centred.

4. **As a dynamic operation, requiring analysis, planning and action.** This view of marketing implies that marketers need to think on their feet and be prepared to change course very rapidly as circumstances dictate. Because customer needs change, and of course new customers are recruited and old ones defect to the competition, marketers will need to be dynamic in their approaches to markets. Equally, competitive responses can force changes on marketers: whatever one firm does, others will either follow or retaliate, so the dynamics of the game are constantly shifting.

5. **As a catalyst for change.** Because marketers operate at the interface between the company and its customers, they frequently act as advocates of the customer's viewpoint, thus making changes within the firm based on customer needs. This means that marketers are expected to be working on behalf of customers to improve the firm's offer and will often find themselves in the position of advising (or seeking to influence) changes within the organisation. Much depends on the position of marketing within the organisation: if marketing is seen as a managerial function rather than the driving force within the organisation, marketers will be one voice among several, supporting the needs of one group of stakeholders (customers) in negotiations with representatives of other groups of stakeholders (employees, shareholders, management and so forth). Internal marketing (the use of marketing techniques to change attitudes and behaviour within the organisation) is linked to this view of marketers as advocates for the customers.

These ways of looking at marketing are not necessarily mutually exclusive. It is possible to view marketing as both an exchange management process and a catalyst for change, for example. Change is managed (for marketers) through a process of advocating an improvement in what is being offered for exchange with customers. Having said that, the idea of marketing as the driving philosophy of the organisation does not sit well with the idea of it being only a managerial function – the 'driving philosophy' view moves marketing to a strategic level, rather than simply a tactical level.

Obtain a copy of your company's mission statement or corporate strategy statement. Where do you think marketing fits into the overall picture? How well does this coincide with your view of where marketing sits within the firm?

If possible, ask some non-marketing colleagues about their views on this – Are we all marketers now or is marketing still a separate function?

CIM exams (and indeed many other exams) are usually based on case studies. Questions are likely to emphasise one or other of the above aspects, even if the examiner does not specifically say so: it is worthwhile considering which aspect is likely to be uppermost in the examiner's mind and ensure that your answer relates to it. Many candidates seem to expect that the case studies are always about companies which are customer-centred, or where marketing occupies a central position, but this is not always the case by any means.

The way to do this is to read the case study carefully first, then decide whether you are being asked to comment on the day-to-day aspects of handling marketing problems (in which case you should think in terms of exchange management, managerial function or dynamic processes) or whether the question is geared more towards strategic issues such as where the company is going in the long term or what objectives are being set (in which case you will be considering the question from the marketing philosophy or catalyst for change aspects).

As you progress through the CIM programmes, you will be expected to take a more strategic approach. You should be aware of this, and be ready to 'change gear', since a very similar question might require a completely different answer at a higher level.

Another view of the development of marketing has been offered by Kotler (2003). This is shown in Figure 1.1.

In Figure 1.1, marketing starts out as being only one of the main four business functions, having equal status. It then moves up to being a more important business function than the others, later evolving to being the most important function and having control over the other functions.

This is not, however, the whole story. In a truly customer-oriented business, the customer will be the driving force for all the business functions: in the final stage of Kotler's view of marketing, the customer becomes central, with marketing acting as the coordinating and integrative function, operating between the customer and the firm.

There is no evidence that this model represents an evolutionary process, but (rather like the evolution of marketing model) it is certainly possible to identify firms which put marketing into those roles.

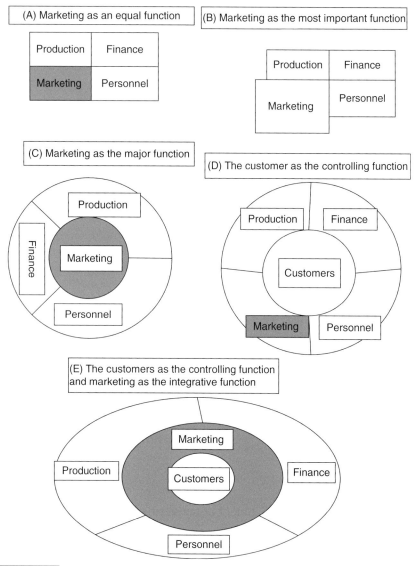

FIGURE 1.1 *Evolution of the role of marketing.*

DIFFICULTIES IN DEVELOPING A MARKETING ORIENTATION

Even though marketers might feel that a market orientation is the obvious way for the firm to go, in practice there are likely to be barriers to developing such an orientation. Some of these come from senior management, some come from colleagues and some are simply the result of organisational inertia. Possible barriers are as follows (See Figure 1.2):

- **Lack of committed leadership and vision.** If the senior management are not on board, it is unlikely that the company can become market-oriented. In some cases, Boards of Directors can be obstructive: partly this is because they have a legal obligation to put shareholders' interests first and may not see the connection between customer orientation and shareholder value, and partly it may arise from ignorance of what marketing is actually about.

- **Lack of customer knowledge.** Clearly it is difficult for firms to become customer oriented if they lack knowledge of their customers. For example, a retailer may not be able to keep good, detailed records of every customer who comes into the shop and may lack the necessary skills or finance to carry out effective market research. In other cases, the customers might be scattered throughout the world, making their purchases via the Internet. In still other cases, customers may not be prepared to tell the marketers about themselves or (worse) may deliberately supply false information – this is not unusual on the Internet where people become worried that information might be misused. Good customer knowledge is basic to establishing a relationship marketing approach.

- **Lack of infrastructure** (e.g. the technology necessary to record and track customer behaviour). This does not necessarily mean that the company cannot be customer oriented, but it may mean that the good

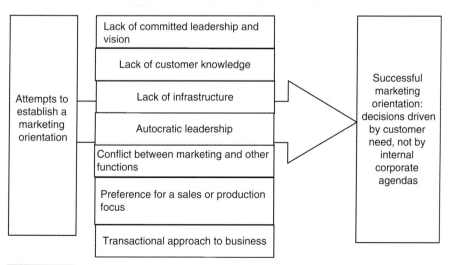

FIGURE 1.2 *Barriers to establishing a marketing orientation.*

intentions are difficult to carry out in practice. The company may also lack the infrastructure to be able to meet customer needs, even when these have been identified: for example, if customers need a rapid delivery service but the road infrastructure of the country does not permit this, the need cannot be met.

- **Autocratic leadership.** A manager who is autocratic is one who wants to make all the decisions himself or herself, based on experience and (of course) power in the organisation. This often acts as a barrier to customer orientation because the market-oriented firm will take its lead from what the customers need, not from what the manager believes is the best way to do things. In other words, the manager is unlikely to be prepared to listen to customers sufficiently.

- **Conflict between marketing and other functions.** In most cases, adopting a market-oriented approach creates problems for other departments. For example, engineering departments are often unwilling to redesign products to suit customer needs, because they believe that it is the job of the marketers to find customers who want to buy the product ('sell what we can make' rather than 'make what we can sell' philosophy). Equally, company finance managers will tend to see customer-based initiatives such as innovative communication campaigns as a cost rather than an investment.

- **Preference for a production or sales focus.** Both these approaches are likely to create quick results: customer orientation takes time to develop and show results, whereas a good salesperson gets results within a few days, and production orientation makes cost savings almost immediately. These approaches are much more easily measured than market orientation, so are often seen as preferable.

- **Transactional approach to business.** If the firm takes the attitude that the sale is the end of the process, a true customer orientation will not happen. For example, very few car dealers ever follow up on a sale once the customer leaves the forecourt, yet a truly customer-oriented dealer would call the customer a couple of months after the car has been sold to check everything is still working properly and would probably also call 2 years or so later to see if the customer is ready to trade the car in. There is more later on about relationship marketing.

Although most firms try to look after their customers, many firms conduct business as if the customers were of no importance except as sources of money: the next section 'Marketing in Practice' provides some examples.

ACTIVITY

In your own firm, make a list of the people who would be most likely to create barriers to the acceptance of a marketing orientation in the firm. What reasons might they have for blocking marketing? Are those reasons justified? How could you overcome their resistance?

Seeing the problem from the other person's viewpoint is something all marketers need to become good at.

The Marketing in Practice box above tells us how NOT to be customer oriented: in the short term, these firms have obviously been fairly successful by using questionable tactics, but in the longer run they will suffer from poor word-of-mouth and customer defection. This is in addition to any penalties or restrictions imposed by the regulators.

MARKETING IN PRACTICE:
Intervention by Regulators

This example shows how some firms exploit customers. Even without the Government regulators, these companies are unlikely to succeed in the long run – customers soon pass the word that they are bad firms to do business with.

In August 2007, the Office of Fair Trading (OFT) announced that it had reached an agreement with an airline regarding price fixing in the long-haul flights market. The airline was to pay a total of £121.5 million as a penalty: the other party to the price fixing was not penalised, because it had come forward to report the price fixing to the OFT. This procedure ensures that it is strongly in the interests of colluding firms to blow the whistle – the other party will be fined, whereas the reporting firm will not and will also have benefitted from the price-fixing arrangement. In September 2009, the OFT imposed fines on six recruitment agencies for price fixing in the construction industry: in 2008 the OFT fined several supermarkets and tobacco manufacturers for price fixing.

Meanwhile, in the voluntary sector, the Advertising Standards Authority (ASA) was also busy. Advanced Hair Studios were told to withdraw an advertisement which implied that their products would grow new hair on balding men, when in fact the effects were merely cosmetic. Agora Lifestyles Ltd. were told to remove an advertisement which implied that their herbal remedies for serious problems such as heart failure and cataracts were being withheld by the medical profession. The ASA ruled that the advertisements could lead people to withdraw from conventional medical treatments – even though Agora pointed out that they were not in fact offering the products for sale, but instead were seeking to sell subscriptions to their health newsletter.

In the same week, the ASA found that an escort agency had breached the regulations by failing to mention that there would be an up-front fee for becoming an escort. The agency concerned mentioned some fees, but not the crucial £350 initial fee: one of the recruits complained after he was not offered any work, despite having paid the fee.

Not all the adjudications went against the advertiser, though. DIY giant Homebase was cleared of misleading advertising when it claimed that prices for garden furniture had been reduced: the complaint had been made by arch-rival B&Q, but was not upheld. A complaint about National Express trains regarding the availability of fares between London and York 'from £13' was also rejected by the ASA, who accepted that the word 'from' would be unlikely to make passengers think that all the tickets would be available at £13.

The ASA, unlike the OFT, has no statutory powers. It cannot force advertisers to comply, and in some cases advertisers have been known to ignore the ASA adjudications. However, the industry as a whole is aware that Government regulation is never far away, so media owners such as newspapers, TV and radio stations and Internet sites comply with ASA rulings, which means that an advertiser who ignores the ASA may well find that there is nowhere for the ads to appear. So far, this sanction has proved very effective and provided everyone acts in a gentlemanly manner; there is no reason why it should not continue to do so.

MARKETING'S CROSS-FUNCTIONAL ROLE

Provided the firm does develop a marketing orientation, marketing will have a role in coordinating all the activities of the firm at every level. Each department, and indeed each individual, should be carrying out his or her role with the customer's welfare in mind. The coordinating role manifests itself in the following ways:

- Information is shared between departments, and interdepartmental relationships are facilitated. For example, market-oriented firms often have a single customer database which contains all the information about any given customer. Non-market-oriented firms often have a separate database for the salesforce, another for the invoicing department, another for the shipping department and so forth. Integrating the databases improves the level of customer service dramatically.

- Common goal setting. Since everything is driven by customer need, the firm can set goals which are measured according to customer-based outcomes. For example, the firm might decide that it needs to reduce customer complaints by 90% and ensure that complaints are satisfactorily dealt with within 48 hours. Since any department in the firm might be subject to a complaint, this type of target will be applied universally.

- Clear company policies can be established regarding products, branding, production, delivery and so forth. All of these impinge on customer satisfaction, and all of them cut across every department in the organisation.

- Marketing becomes a service provider. The marketing department should be offering services to all departments, for example, providing information about the market to engineers developing new products, advising the finance department on the best way to approach slow payers, talking to the delivery people about providing a better service for customers and so forth.

- Marketing contributes to strategic planning. Strategy in business is about developing competitive advantage. Marketing offers the opportunity to develop competitive advantage through superior customer value, and although there may be other ways of developing advantage (e.g. by reducing costs dramatically), a good understanding of customer need is difficult to copy: customers are almost always prepared to pay more for a better product or service.

- Internal marketing becomes an important aspect of the marketing function.

ACTIVITY

List the people from other departments who are affected by what the marketing people in your firm do. Which people are adversely affected by marketing activities? Which are affected positively by what marketing does?

How might you lessen the impact on those adversely affected, bearing in mind their own needs both in their jobs and as individuals, and also bearing in mind the need for marketing to achieve its own objectives? How might you win them over to your cause?

CASE STUDY: Legoland

This case study illustrates how customer orientation acts as a coordinating theme for a company's activities and as a central focus. It also shows how resistance to marketing (in this case, the resistance comes from retailers) can be addressed.

Fifty years ago, the children's toy market was invaded by a little plastic brick with eight studs on it. The studs enabled the bricks to stick together, and soon millions of children were playing with Lego – the old wooden building bricks that children had played with for centuries were doomed to remain at the bottom of the toy cupboard.

Lego has moved on from strength to strength – the Legoland theme park in Denmark was followed by another one in the United Kingdom, at Windsor, to the west of London. Lego brand was extending beyond its core business – and the man in charge of licensing the Lego brand, Karl Kalcher, had even bigger ideas in store.

In 1999, Kalcher opened the first Lego store in Britain, at the Bluewater shopping complex in Kent, not far from the Channel Tunnel. Kalcher is a champion of innovative thinking in marketing, something which has led to his becoming a Fellow of the United Kindom's Chartered Institute of Marketing. He is famous for saying 'There's no such thing as children. It doesn't mean anything.'

This statement sounds a little odd from a man whose company targets the 0–16 age group, but in fact what he says makes perfect sense: there is a vast difference between a 3-year-old and a 12-year-old, and even between a 3-year-old and a 5-year-old. Kalcher says that there are only consumers – each with a separate personality and separate needs.

Lego Licensing licenses watches, clothing, the Lego Island CD-ROM and of course the Legoland theme parks. The Lego group plans to become the leading brand among families and children, which means doing a lot more than moulding eight-stud plastic bricks. The Lego store is set to help in this bold ambition. The store is designed to be as user-friendly as possible for its diminutive customers – the store adheres to the 'Lego values', and these were referred to throughout the design and construction of the store. Beginning with the store front, Lego decided that the company's heritage lay in design and construction – so the store front is designed around the colours and proportions of the Lego bricks. Lego is a toy, so the interior of the store is a high-touch environment – customers are actively encouraged to touch things and play with things, but since Lego is also an educational toy, much of what happens in the store is also educational. For example, there is a 'rocket-race' game in which children have to memorise a number in order to make the rocket fly. Many of the displays are at children's eye level, so that children can use the store without adult intervention (until it comes time to pay, of course).

Finally, the Lego store has impressive giant Lego models in the window area, which, according to Lego's retail boss Paul Denham, creates the 'wow' factor. Kalcher believes that, in creating the store, he is setting a standard of innovation that retailers alone would be unable to aspire to. He believes that it is up to the brand owners to invest time and trouble in extending the brand into new areas such as retailing: traditional retailers are, in effect, unable to achieve these standards.

Not unnaturally, retailers in the area objected strongly to the establishment of the Lego store. As long-term Lego stockists, they felt that their loyalty had been betrayed, and they feared that Lego would also undercut them on price. In fact, these fears proved groundless. Kalcher explains why: 'The Lego store is essentially about creating a superior standard for our brand, in the eyes of the consumer. This will promote the esteem of our products for all retail customers.' Kalcher could be confident in making this statement – sales were actually boosted in retailers near Lego's Minneapolis store and near Legoland Windsor. And as regards price cutting, the Lego stores are stand-alone franchised outlets – they operate under the same constraints as any other retailer, so they have to show a profit, which means no price-cutting.

Lego has come a long way in 50 years, but it has a reputation for quality and for getting it right – so much so that, even before there was any hint of Lego opening a store at Bluewater, the developers had used Legoland Windsor as a benchmark for designing the entire shopping centre. Lego now has 80% of the world's construction toy market and expects to build even further successes around the other elements of the brand.

Questions

1. What is Lego doing that most of its competitors are not doing?

2. Lego's consumers are children, but the customers are the parents. How does Lego address this?

3. What is the coordinating role of Lego's approach?

4. How is Lego using its marketing philosophy to expand the business?

INTERNAL MARKETING

Internal marketing is the use of the tools of marketing to create a suitable organisational culture, usually one which places the customer at the centre of what the firm does. Internal marketing should aim to achieve the following outcomes:

1. Encourage an atmosphere of pride. This might involve highlighting the achievements of individuals (perhaps as Employee of the Month) and publicising these to others in the organisation, or perhaps empowering innovative staff to become agents of change.

2. Provide suitable vehicles for innovation. Communication channels should be established which enable innovative ideas to be disseminated and discussed across departmental boundaries. Weblogs, discussion forums and newsletters can be powerful in achieving this type of outcome.

3. Improve lateral communication. Encouraging joint project teams and working groups, encouraging interdepartmental social events and exchanging people between departments on temporary secondments wherever possible will help here.

4. Cut down layers of hierarchy. Empowering staff at 'grass roots' level will mean that customer needs will be met more efficiently, especially in the case of complaint handling. Employees tend to feel more motivated if they have more control over what happens in the firm.

5. Increase the available information about company plans and projects. Obviously there will be some plans which will be commercially sensitive, and of use to competitors, so not everything can be publicised to staff. However, it is clearly beneficial if staff understand how the company plans to achieve its strategic objectives, and internal marketing will help in ensuring that everyone knows which direction the firm is going in. This will reduce errors and duplication of effort as well as ensure that everyone is aware of what they should be doing at any given time.

6. Ensure that the leadership is aware of its limited perspective. Senior managers can easily lose touch with the day-to-day reality of work at the 'grass roots' level. Even though most of them will have worked their way up from the lower ranks, they may be unaware of how the environment has changed. Internal marketing should help to facilitate communications between people working with customers and senior managers at the top of the firm.

Internal marketing uses similar tools to customer-based marketing. It begins by recognising that the exchange between employer and employee goes far beyond simply exchanging hours or work for money: there is considerable emotional labour involved in the workplace. People talk about their work when they go home, feel involved with the organisation, feel proud when their organisation does something they approve of and feel ashamed when their organisation does something they do not approve of.

Typical internal marketing tools are as follows:

1. **Internal newsletters.** These can take the form of notice boards, e-mail attachments or even a simple A4 sheet of paper with the latest company information on them.

2. **Staff magazines.** These can be glossy magazines with articles about employees, articles of general interest and even advertising – employees who want to sell unwanted goods, invite people to a social event or even publicise their out-of-office hobbies might want to advertise. Often these advertisements will be the main reason for staff reading the magazine, so these can be a powerful addition to the staff magazine.

3. **Staff meetings.** Meetings can often be extremely boring, but a meeting between staff members and senior managers to raise issues, hand out praise or simply communicate new policies can be a powerful tool. Such meetings can be conducted in an informal manner – the organisation might provide a buffet or arrange for the meeting to be held in a conference room away from the firm. Both these techniques reduce the barriers between senior managers and staff.

4. **Team-building exercises.** These can be particularly important when inducting new people into the organisation. The company can set up games or challenges to encourage people to understand each others' approach to problem-solving or can form groups such as quality circles across departmental boundaries to work on specific projects.

5. **Awards for employees.** Employee of the Month awards are often used, but small prizes or gifts for exceptional performance can be offered at any time, particularly if a staff member has facilitated a successful new idea. Some firms have suggestion schemes which pay cash rewards for successful ideas – many motor manufacturers

do this, as it is often the case that a production line worker will recognise a recurring problem much faster than a design engineer who rarely works on the line.

Internal marketing is an important, and sometimes neglected, aspect of marketing. Helping to build a successful, dynamic corporate culture is a key factor in creating a successful, dynamic corporation.

THE IMPACT OF MARKETING ON SOCIETY, CONSUMERS AND ENVIRONMENT

EXAM HINT

You are likely to be asked a specific question on ethics or societal marketing (see below) and it is likely that you will gain marks by bearing in mind any ethical issues raised within case studies. In particular, you should consider the ethical issues implied by any recommendations you make in your answers.

Since you will have at least some questions with a global element in them, you will need to consider ethics in a global sense, not just in terms of your own country's morality.

Anybody who works in marketing has had the annoying experience of being accused of creating needs, persuading people to buy things they do not need or want and of being anti-environmentalist. Business generally has a bad reputation in some quarters, and marketers often bear the brunt of people's complaints about the system.

In recent years, the concept of corporate social responsibility has come to the forefront of business thinking, particularly for marketers since they are at the interface between the firm and its customers. Corporate social responsibility implies that firms should behave ethically and responsibly, avoiding damage to the environment or to the society at large. For marketers, this view has become encapsulated in the concept of societal marketing. Societal marketing questions whether the marketing concept is sufficient in a world of resource shortages, pollution problems and poverty.

Societal marketing aims to balance the needs of consumers, society and the company so as to meet the corporate and consumer needs without damaging the interests of society at large. The balance is difficult to maintain – as the Marketing in Practice example below shows.

MARKETING IN PRACTICE:
Bhopal

This example illustrates the complexity of dealing with ethical issues at a practical level. At first sight, this is a clear case of corporate negligence – but identifying the culprit, and possibly even the victims, is not so simple.

On 2 December 1984, over 40 tons of lethal chemical gas was released into the air from the Union Carbide chemical factory in Bhopal, India. The accident was caused by water entering a tank containing chemicals: the resulting chemical reaction generated great heat and vented the poisonous gases into the atmosphere. As a result, thousands of people in the area were killed – estimates vary between 3,800 and 8,000 – and hundreds of thousands have suffered ill health ever since.

Union Carbide was held accountable by the world's press, and the company was widely criticised by environmental groups. Union Carbide was seen as being slow to pay compensation, slow to make reparations at the plant and slow to implement a clean-up operation. Often, the American parent company was accused of not caring simply because the victims were Indians.

Union Carbide have pointed out that only 51% of the plant was owned by the company, the rest being owned by the Indian Government (26%) and private shareholders (23%). The Bhopal plant was staffed and managed entirely by Indians. In 1989, an Indian court ordered Union Carbide to pay $470 million in damages, in full and final settlement, and the company did so, but the trouble has not gone away: campaigners say that birth defects in the area are caused by chemicals from the plant. This is denied by Union Carbide, who say that soil contamination is caused by chemicals which were never used at the plant and that close interbreeding (a feature of marriages in the Bhopal area) is what is causing the birth defects. The US company denies any liability whatsoever and has the backing of the Second Circuit Court of Appeals in Manhattan, which ruled in 1987 that the case belongs solely in India and the US company has no liability whatsoever. The Indian Government was held partly liable and has bought health insurance for the 100,000 people who are thought to have been affected, but since the original $470 million was paid to the Indian Government to administer rather than go directly to the victims, this insurance was paid for from the money Union Carbide had already paid out. The Indian Government did not release the remainder of the funds until 2005, over 20 years after the accident happened.

In 1998, the Madhya Pradesh State Government took over responsibility for cleaning up the site, but there is some doubt that any actual clean-up has happened since. Union Carbide's investigators concluded that the original accident was no accident – they found that it could only have been caused by deliberate sabotage. According to Union Carbide, this finding was backed up by independent Indian Government inspectors.

The case has since become even more complicated: in 2001, Dow Chemical bought Union Carbide. Dow, understandably, do not feel any responsibility whatever for Bhopal and are refusing to consider any further claims. Meanwhile, campaigners have persuaded an Indian court to issue a warrant for the arrest of Union Carbide's former CEO, Warren Anderson, on charges of culpable homicide. Anderson is unlikely to be extradited from the United States, but probably should not visit India any time soon. According to campaigners, Union Carbide kept potentially life-saving information about the effects of the gases secret, since it was 'commercially sensitive', and they also accuse the company of leaving sacks of damaging chemicals at the factory site.

While this high-level wrangling goes on, the survivors of Bhopal wait. The case has dragged on for a quarter of a century: the compensation worked out to only $500 each, which may be a lot of money to someone who only earns $2 a day, but still will not cover the medical bills. Union Carbide (India) is now owned by an entirely different company, which (like Dow in the United States) feels no responsibility for the disaster. The campaigning continues, however, presumably until the last of the survivors has died – in 2007, a case was filed in the United States holding Union Carbide and Warren Anderson liable for pollution of neighbouring properties, but like the other claims against the US company, this is unlikely to succeed.

As the case shows, Union Carbide has paid out substantial compensation, as has the Indian Government. For Union Carbide (and now Dow Chemical), paying out any more would be a violation of the trust their shareholders have placed in the company: after all, it is not the Board of Directors' own money, but belongs to the shareholders. Legally and morally, the company believes itself to be in the right – but this does not help the people who have suffered, and continue to suffer, as a result of the accident.

The societal marketing concept remains an issue which excites considerable academic and practitioner debate, since it expands the role of marketing to include everybody in the world, not just customers and consumers. There is a question about whether companies are justified in using shareholders' money for social purposes and a question about where to draw the line: should companies simply stay within the law and rely on government to set the appropriate rules, should companies and trade organisations (such as the CIM) set codes of practice or should managers and directors obey some higher moral code?

CASE STUDY: Bribery and Big Business

This case study is about bribery and the conflict between managing shareholders' money to best effect on the one hand and taking a moral stance on the other. Bribery is clearly endemic in some business cultures, while in others it is regarded as seriously immoral, which adds to the problem.

Lockheed is one of the world's largest aircraft manufacturers and therefore conducts business throughout the world. Though primarily a military aircraft manufacturer (producing the F1-11 fighter and the Galaxy transport plane), Lockheed also produced the TriStar commercial aircraft, until 1983 when the company left the commercial aircraft business permanently.

In 1976, Lockheed revealed that it had paid out over $22 million in 'sales commissions' to foreign Government officials, including $1 million to Prince Bernhard of the Netherlands in exchange for doing business with Lockheed. Although there was some doubt at the time as to whether these were bribes or payments extorted by the officials under threat of cancelling orders, several senior Lockheed executives were forced to resign, and a shocked US Government passed legislation outlawing such practices even when they occurred outside the United States.

Unfortunately, the legislation seems to have done little to prevent bribery from happening. Lockheed have been fined (in 1995) for bribing the Egyptian government, General Electric were fined for diverting funds from the Military Aid Program to finance the sale of aircraft engines to Israel and in 2000 Boeing were fined for exporting arms to Turkey. It seems that the only way to do business in some countries is to pay 'commissions' or to 'grease the wheels' even if this does violate the law. In fact, the US Government even ignores its own policies on the issue of corruption by continuing to give contracts to these companies – but of course they have little choice in practice, unless they took the bizarre step of placing defence contracts with foreign suppliers.

Ultimately, the morality of bribery is not in question, even in countries where it is rife. Bribery is immoral and in most cases illegal. It is damaging to the business, to the countries where it happens and to the people who give and accept the bribes. Yet it still goes on, because immediate gain often outweighs long-term disadvantages – especially when the stakes are as high as they are in the aircraft industry.

Questions

1. Why should not Lockheed continue to offer bribes in countries where this is normal business practice?

2. How might governments stop bribery from happening?

3. Is bribery an appropriate use of shareholders' money?

4. Why is bribery damaging?

Business morality is driven by three main influences (See Figure 1.3):

1. **Codes of practice such as the CIM code.** These are voluntary sets of rules drawn up by trade bodies and are policed by the trade bodies themselves. They do not usually have a legal status, but they would certainly be taken into account in the event of any legal action taken by an outside party. Sanctions against violators can include having membership of the trade body cancelled, which may or may not have serious effects but would certainly be embarrassing.

2. **Legal constraints.** Corporate citizenship involves upholding the law and behaving responsibly, so firms need to be aware of the legal implications of their actions. This can be complex for companies operating globally, since they not only have to take account of different laws in different countries, but also have to work within different legal systems (e.g. the American system and the Japanese system are entirely different, so that contracts have an entirely different status and meaning in each country). For this reason, international contracts usually specify which jurisdiction will be used for settling any disputes.

3. **Local morals and customs.** This is, again, a minefield for the global company, since morality is not universal (as the Lockheed case study shows). What is moral does not necessarily equate to what is legal, further complicating the issue – this is yet another potential source of

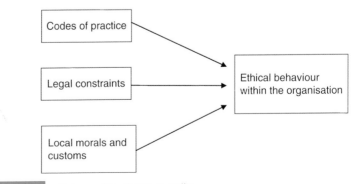

FIGURE 1.3 *Drivers of business morality.*

conflict within the firm, as the legal department concentrates on legality while the marketers consider wider moral and cultural issues.

STUDY TIP

You will be expected to understand the social issues surrounding business activities, so you should read some of the anti-business, anti-global, anti-marketing literature. You should also be aware of the activities of pressure groups such as Greenpeace and Friends of the Earth: since these are regularly reported in the news, you should try to stay abreast of developments. Visiting their websites will allow you to understand their point of view – but remember that websites only ever give one side of the story!

A general point here is that you are studying for a vocational qualification: you should always be applying what you have learned to what you read in the newspapers or online.

ACTIVITY

Obtain copies of some trade codes of practice. If you have one for your own industry, compare it with the CIM code of practice or with other codes of practice. What are the similarities? What are the differences? What sanctions can be applied to violators?

In the case of comparing the CIM code with the industry code, are there any areas where there might be conflicts, that is, points at which following one code would bring you into conflict with another?

To what extent do you think codes of practice are actually followed in the real world?

RELATIONSHIP MARKETING VERSUS TRANSACTIONAL MARKETING

EXAM HINT

Because relationship marketing is so important in marketing thinking, it is likely to pervade any exam question even if this is not specifically stated. Any recommendations you make should be made in the light of trying to establish customer loyalty.

The concept of relationship marketing has been at the forefront of marketing debate for the last 20 years or more. The basis of relationship marketing is the concept that it is cheaper, easier and more profitable to retain existing customers than it is to recruit new ones, so the general aim of relationship marketing is to minimise customer 'churn' (the rate at which customers are lost to competitors and replaced by new ones) and to establish a long-term business relationship with customers.

ACTIVITY

Anybody working in marketing quickly becomes aware that some customers just are not worth keeping. They are troublesome, are expensive to deal with or simply do not spend enough money to be worth the effort.

Find out what your company does to retain customers. Are there mechanisms in place for recovering defecting customers? If so, what discrimination is made (if any) between customers who are worth recovering and those who should be allowed to go because retaining them would be too expensive or troublesome? If there is no system for retention, what could be done to develop such a system? How would you discriminate between customers who are worth retaining and those who are not?

Relationship marketing has the following drivers:

- Retaining customers is cheaper than recruiting new ones. This is debatable: much depends on the relative costs of retention and acquisition, but for firms where acquisition costs are high this would certainly be true. Usually, this will be the case if the value of goods is high, or in the case of business-to-business transactions.

- Customer defection is damaging to the company. If customers leave, they may do so as a result of dissatisfaction, in which case they are likely to generate negative word-of-mouth. Also, if they continue to buy similar products to our own, they will be helping to fund a competitor.

- Customer loyalty leads to long-term stability and growth. If we have a core of loyal customers, it is much easier to predict revenues, and recruiting new customers will lead to growth.

- Technological advances allow firms to keep much more detailed information about customers and enable marketers to determine (and meet) customer needs more effectively. For example, in Victorian times shopkeepers would know their customers personally, but for a modern supermarket chain this would be impossible without using computers and loyalty cards.

- Customers should be judged on their lifetime value, not just on the value of the individual transaction. The danger here, especially in business to consumer markets, is that the firm will tend to target younger people, ignoring older consumers who probably have more money. Lifetime value is a key concept in relationship marketing: a customer who spends relatively little but remains loyal for many years is likely to generate a great deal more revenue and profit for the company than a customer who spends a large amount, but quickly defects to a competitor.

- Small changes in retention rates have large effects of future revenues. The research evidence for this is strong – quite a minor improvement in retention, as little as 1%, has been shown to increase a firm's value by around 5% (Gupta et al. 2004). Other studies have shown similar benefits – a study undertaken by the Cumberland Bank in the United States showed that a 5% improvement in retention of the bank's top customers added 4% to the bank's profitability.

Having said that, not every customer is worth retaining, and not every firm finds that the benefits outweigh the costs of building the relationship.

STUDY TIP

It is worthwhile familiarising yourself with the arguments against relationship marketing: the jury is still out on the effectiveness of the approach, especially in terms of business-to-consumer situations. For relationships to work, both parties need to be prepared to adapt: many firms are unable or unwilling to do this, and certainly few consumers are prepared to.

In practice, establishing and managing relationships require a different mindset from that used in a traditional, transactional approach. Table 1 makes the comparison between relationship marketing and transactional marketing.

Table 1.1 Transactional marketing vs. relationship marketing

Transactional marketing	Relationship marketing
Focus on single sale	Focus on customer retention
Orientation on product features	Orientation on product benefits
Short timescale	Long timescale
Little emphasis on customer service	High emphasis on customer service
Limited customer commitment	High customer commitment
Moderate customer contact	High customer contact
Quality is the concern of the production department	Quality is the concern of all

Source: Christopher, M., Ballantyne, D. and Payne, A. (1991) *Relationship Marketing*, Oxford: Butterworth-Heinemann.

Relationship marketing has generally been more successful in business-to-business markets than in business-to-consumer markets. There may be several reasons for this. Some are as follows:

1. Business needs change a great deal more slowly than consumer needs. A consumer who is loyal to a baby product such as Pampers will not need the product once the baby is out of nappies, so the maximum lifetime value of the customer is probably around 2 years.

2. Consumers see little benefit in establishing a relationship with a supplier, whereas a business buyer gains a great deal from establishing a good working relationship with suppliers.

3. Good relationships depend on goodwill and trust, and consumers tend not to trust businesses.

CASE STUDY: União Digital Periféricos LTDA

This case study illustrates the difficulty of maintaining good customer relationships over long distances and in conditions where the infrastructure might be poor. This company has needed to be innovative in its approach to relationship marketing.

In 1989, Brazil opened its doors to trade liberalisation. Until then, many imports had been so heavily taxed that they were effectively excluded from the ailing Brazilian economy: in the case of computer imports, this restriction almost proved fatal. When American and Japanese computer systems arrived in Brazil, the country's own systems were so far behind the times that the economy was severely affected.

In the intervening years, however, Brazil has made incredible progress in catching up with computer technology. This has opened up a huge market for components and software – and União Digital Periféricos LTDA has taken full advantage of the rapid growth in demand. The company concluded distribution agreements with Compaq, Flextronics Semiconductors, OPTi Inc. and many other multinational and global firms. In 2000, the company set up a joint venture with Nokia to establish a seamless remote connection system providing secure connections between the Internet, intranets and extranets: the system operates nationwide for remote business, and the solution was expected to cost around $20 million. União Digital is now among the largest distributors of electronic components in South America, distributing throughout the Mercosul countries.

União Digital supplies a complete range of products for LAN and WAN and (given the rapid growth of computer-based systems in Brazil over the last 15 years or so) now supplies, or has supplied, virtually every major company in Brazil. The company always adds value to its products – it supplies training, system design and after-sales technical assistance. This level of service is important in a country where computer literacy has only recently been on the agenda.

Brazil is the largest country in South America – as large as the United States or Australia, with a population of 140 million, Brazil is also the industrial powerhouse of the continent, particularly in the South. This means that União Digital has a problem retaining its relationships with customers who may be thousands of miles from the company's São Paulo base. To help solve the problem, União Digital called in international business consultants BearingPoint to revamp the company's website with the express purpose of improving customer retention and relationships.

BearingPoint reconstructed the already-effective União Digital website in order to increase the personalisation and one-to-one marketing capability of the site. The site allows customers access to news and information which is tailored to the customer's precise profile – this eliminates the need for customers to plough through masses of irrelevant information in order to find the particular information they need. BearingPoint used its alliance with Cisco Systems to carry out the project.

As one of the key features of the solution, União Digital has incorporated its new price policy, whereby pricing varies by client and is based on individual purchasing volumes, future opportunities, technical certification and reseller's performance. In addition, resellers will have the ability to publish their own marketing information through the União Digital website. The website will also be integrated with Cisco Systems' website to allow clients to purchase and configure Cisco products from the União Digital website.

BearingPoint was originally KPMG Consulting, but after acquiring the Andersen consultancy business, the name was changed and the new company was formed. The company's worldwide perspective, and its ability to bring numerous international alliances to bear, was crucial in its thinking on União Digital. BearingPoint has a large network of suppliers and customers (some of whom are both at different times) and was able to use its network to develop a creative and effective solution for União Digital.

In a society where personal relationships are important, União Digital has managed to create an impressive set of business relationships. The company is able to use its website to support and even build on those relationships – the key to its long-term success in a growing market.

Questions

1. Why are relationships so important for União Digital?

2. Why would the company use the impersonal medium of a website to improve its relationships rather than spend more effort and money on personal contacts via salespeople?

3. What role did BearingPoint's relationship marketing have in the process?

4. How might União Digital further improve its relationship marketing?

5. What are the specific advantages for União Digital in retaining customers?

Undoubtedly, relationship marketing has a great deal to offer, and the general thinking behind it is the basis for key account management, database marketing and much of the direct marketing that you will learn about later in the course. Making it work in practice is, however, somewhat more problematical.

Many marketers think that providing a good product and a good back-up service is enough to create customer loyalty, whereas in fact this is far from being the case. The purpose of relationship marketing is to establish a true dialogue with customers so that they become 'locked into' the supplier. On a small scale, restaurants and some retailers such as family butchers establish relationships with regular customers. This has nothing to do with offering lower prices or better food than competitors, but it has everything to do with knowing the customer's name, knowing their individual tastes and preferences and knowing their likely spending power. A butcher who can greet a customer by name, tell him or her that a special cut of meat will be available and sometimes do a special deal for a customer will create loyalty. Likewise, a restaurateur who can offer a customer 'the usual, Mr. and Mrs. Smith?' will generate a sense of being 'a friend in the business' rather than someone who is simply looking to show a profit.

The difficulty for relationship marketers is to translate this small-business capability into a large-business scenario. Major supermarkets create this sense of dialogue by offering loyalty cards. At first, the data collected from loyalty card records were used to promote products that the customer currently was not buying. This proved counter-productive, because people have many reasons for not buying something, but it usually boils down to one overwhelmingly obvious reason – they do not want the product. Supermarkets then went on to analysing customer purchases and offering items which were specifically tailored to the individual; for example, promoting home-baking products to someone who has shown, by his or her purchasing pattern, to be keen on baking at home.

Small gifts can be helpful, but in general firms do well to show that they have a sympathy for the customer and are looking for ways to make life easier. For example, before Christmas 2009, Tesco sent out the Clubcard rewards early: instead of them coming out at the end of January, the supermarket sent them out so that people could take advantage of them at Christmas, which is of course an expensive time of year for most people. Having the vouchers virtually ensured that people would do their Christmas shopping in Tesco's rather than at any other supermarket.

ACTIVITY

Make a list of your best customers. This should be about 20% of your customers overall (if you work in a B2C company this may be difficult to assess, of course). Approximately how much of your firm's sales do these customers account for?

Now calculate what would happen if they defected to your competitors. How would your company survive? Could it survive?

Finally, think about what you would need to do to ensure that each of these customers remains with your firm. What can you do for each of them, individually or collectively, that would tend to lock them into your company?

SEGMENTATION, TARGETING AND POSITIONING

Although segmentation, targeting and positioning are not part of the *Marketing Essentials* syllabus, and you will not be expected to answer questions about these aspects of marketing, it may be helpful to have a brief outline of what they are since they are fundamental to the concept of meeting customer need.

Segmentation is the process of dividing the overall market into groups of people with similar needs. For example, the car market comprises a very large number of different types of people: in Western Europe and the

United States it might be considered to be the entire population. Within that overall market, however, there are many subgroups: people who need a small, economical car for city driving, people who need a luxury car, people who need a car for long-distance driving (sales people, for example), people who need a car with off-road capability and so forth. It would be impossible to produce one car that would suit all these different people, so manufacturers divide the market into segments, each with similar needs and wants.

Segments are typically defined by demographic factors (age, wealth, family life stage, etc.), by geographical factors (climate, terrain, country of residence), by behavioural factors (the way they use the product, purchase behaviour, etc.) or by psychographic factors (attitudes to the company and product category, specific fears or desires, personal motivations). No single segmentation factor is adequate, though – for example, segmenting a market by age is extremely unreliable since people do not always 'act their age', whereas segmenting by age and by attitude can be extremely revealing.

Having decided how the market breaks down, marketers are in a position to choose which segment or segments the company can serve best. This decision, the targeting decision, is made by matching up what the company is capable of doing, against the needs and wants of the segment. In many cases, a segment which would be very profitable (or which would be strategically important) has to be passed up because the company cannot meet the needs of the segment. In other cases, segments which have been ignored by other, perhaps larger, firms are easily served by the company. In general, the more tightly defined the segment is, the more their needs converge and the more likely it is that they will be prepared to pay a premium price for the 'ideal' product.

Finally, positioning is the process of communicating the brand to the target customers in such a way that they can easily recognise where it fits with competing products. Positioning may be achieved in terms of price, quality, reliability, availability, exclusiveness or any of several hundred factors. Sometimes brands are positioned in psychological terms: whether a particular brand of trainers is 'cool' or not will determine its position, and some people are certainly loyal to particular motor manufacturers, switching between different models as their needs change.

In Figure 1.4, the overall vehicle market is shown as breaking down into a number of product categories. A company with a particular capability in producing off-road vehicles might segment its market as landowners (farmers, etc.), recreational drivers such as mountain climbers or canoeists who may need to drive their equipment and friends to remote locations, and fashionable city dwellers who like to drive a big four-wheel drive vehicle. The respective positions for the product are shown: note

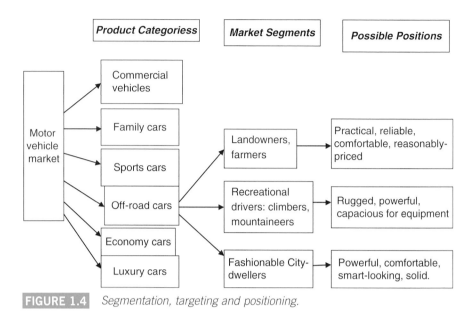

FIGURE 1.4 *Segmentation, targeting and positioning.*

that each end user will have a different idea of what is a desirable position for their purchase.

SUMMARY

Marketing is a young discipline: it has its roots in economics, psychology, sociology, salesmanship and many other areas, but it has gone through a rapid evolution to reach the current state of the art. As a dynamic process of continual re-invention, academic marketing has paralleled developments in day-to-day practice, moving the profession from a somewhat dubious commercial practice to a means by which people meet their daily needs and life aspirations.

The key points from this section are as follows:

- Marketing has gone through a number of stages to reach its present place as the primary means of managing exchange.

- Marketing creates competitive advantage by first creating customer value.

- Marketing orientation can only be developed with the co-operation of all members of the organisation.

- Marketing orientation can be met with resistance from people within the firm.

- True marketing orientation cuts across departments within the firm.

- Marketing has a role in maintaining ethical standards, and marketers need to be aware of the effects of marketing activities on the well-being of the society as a whole.

- Relationship marketing is concerned with establishing long-term exchange patterns with appropriate customers.

SELF-CHECK QUESTIONS

1. Which of the following is true?

   A In a transactional marketing environment, quality is the responsibility of everyone in the firm.

   B In a relationship marketing environment, there is a high emphasis on customer service.

   C In a transactional marketing environment, the focus is on the long term.

2. Which of the following is a stage in marketing evolution?

   A Product orientation.

   B Orientation on product benefits.

   C Quality control.

3. Which of the following is true?

   A Product orientation came before production orientation and after sales orientation.

  B Sales orientation came after production orientation but before marketing orientation.

  C Production orientation came after product orientation and before sales orientation.

4. Lack of committed leadership:

  A Creates production orientation.

  B Hinders marketing orientation.

  C Promotes sales orientation.

5. Common goal setting is an example of:

  A Marketing's ability to generate cross-functional coordination.

  B Production orientation.

  C Relationship marketing.

FURTHER READING

Chapter 1 of *Essentials of Marketing* (Blythe, J., 4th Edition: Harlow, Pearson). Alternatively, Chapter 1 of *Principles of Marketing* (Blythe, J., 2nd Edition: Andover, Cengage), Chapter 1 of *Principles of Marketing* (Brassington, F., and Pettitt, S., 4th Edition: Harlow, FT Prentice Hall), Chapter 1 of *Principles of Marketing* (Kotler et al.), *Principles and Practice of Marketing* (Jobber, D., 6th Edition: Maidenhead, McGraw Hill). Jobber approaches the question in a somewhat different way which does not fit the CIM syllabus.

  The CIM Code of Practice.

JOURNAL ARTICLES

Anderson, E.W., Fornell, C. and Mazvancheryl, S.K. (2004): Customer satisfaction and shareholder value. *Journal of Marketing*, **68**(4), 172–185.

Avlonitis, G. et al., (1997): Marketing orientation and company performance: industrial vs. consumer goods companies. *Industrial Marketing Management*, **26**(5): 385–402.

Homburg, C., Koschate, N. and Hoyer, W.D. (2005): Do satisfied customers really pay more? A study of the relationship between customer satisfaction and willingness to pay. *Journal of Marketing*, **69**(2): 84–96.

Narver, J.C. and Slater, S.F. (1990): The effects of a market orientation on business profitability. *Journal of Marketing*, **54**(October): 20–55.

WEBSITES

www.cim.co.uk (for CIM code of practice)

http://www.btplc.com/Thegroup/Regulatoryinformation/Codeofpractice/Consu mercodeofpractice/ConsumerCodeofPractice.htm (example of a code of practice)

http://www.imc.co.uk/news/professional_consultancy_article.php?item_ id=427&issue=13 (articles on how marketing can be integrated into the business philosophy)

CHAPTER 2

Planning within the Marketing Context

Learning objectives

After working through this module and reading around the subject, you should be able to

- Explain the importance of objectives, the processes for setting them and the influences upon them.
- Identify the various possible organisational objectives.
- Show how marketing planning is crucial in a market-oriented organisation.
- Describe the stages of the marketing planning process.
- Explain the concept of the marketing audit.

SETTING OBJECTIVES

First, we need to distinguish between an aim and an objective. An aim is simply a statement of something we would like to do, for example, the firm might aim to be the best-respected in the industry, or we might aim for our promotional campaigns to be more memorable. These are not objectives. An objective is an aim which is measurable, that is, we have some means of knowing that we achieved the objective. Statements such as 'we wish to sell as much as possible' are aims, not objectives, because we have no real way of knowing how much 'as much as possible' actually is.

Objectives are the building blocks of strategy. They are the basis for determining future direction, consistency, motivation and measurement of performance.

EXAM TIP

You will often be asked to make recommendations for future action for a firm. You will gain marks if you think in terms of setting objectives for your recommendations, because this will make them more concrete.

For example, if you are asked to suggest ways in which a firm might enter an overseas market, it is of no help to say 'the firm should investigate the local culture further'.

A recommendation would include an objective such as 'the firm should commission a local agency to report on the acceptability of the firm's products, the report to be completed within 3 months. The report should also indicate the size of the potential market, stated as a percentage of the population'. Put this way, the senior managers have a solid course of action to follow.

An objective should be SMART, that is, it should be:

1. **Specific.** This means that it should be possible to state it in precise terms, in such a way that it cannot be confused with any other action. If an objective is not clearly stated, it becomes open to interpretation by those who have to carry out the necessary actions to achieve it. In some cases this simply leads to misunderstanding and wasted effort, but in more serious cases it can leave the way open for people to work to their own agendas, using the objective as a way of justifying their actions.

2. **Measurable.** There should be some kind of numerical or other measure to quantify the objective. Without this, we cannot know whether the objective has been achieved. Over-achievement can be as serious as under-achievement: sometimes over-achieving a sales objective leads to problems in meeting demand, which can result in a loss of goodwill towards the firm. For example, a flying school which over-achieves its objectives for attracting new customers might find that it does not have enough aircraft and instructors to meet the demand, leading to disappointment among the would-be aviators.

3. **Achievable.** If an objective cannot be achieved, there is little point in setting it. Objectives which are perceived by employees and others to be unachievable will simply be ignored: worse, employees will have

less respect for management as a result and be less likely to believe in future objectives.

4. **Realistic.** Following on from the criterion of being achievable, an objective needs to make sense within the context of the firm's situation and strategy. If the objective does not connect with other objectives in the strategy, it is unlikely to be achieved, and even if it is achieved it will not contribute anything to the firm's success.

5. **Timebound.** There should always be a point at which the managers can say that the objective has not been achieved. If there is no timescale, people can continue to try for the objective indefinitely, which is of course a pointless state of affairs.

For example, if we have an aim that our promotional campaigns should be more memorable, this can only become an objective if we are able to map it against SMART, perhaps as follows:

- **Specific.** We would like 30% of respondents to name our brand in an unaided recall test.

- **Measurable.** We will be commissioning a market research organisation to carry out the recall test.

- **Achievable.** Our campaign last year resulted in 20% unaided recall, so this campaign should be able to improve on that.

- **Realistic.** 30% unaided recall is well within what other brands in our portfolio have achieved, and we would expect this brand to achieve this if it is to remain in the portfolio.

- **Timebound.** We are allowing a 3-month time frame for the campaign to have its effect.

Obviously, there will be a degree of overlap between the various SMART factors, but if even one of them is not present the objective is not viable.

STUDY TIP

Within your own work environment or working day, try analysing your day's objectives against SMART factors. This will help you remember them more clearly and will also provide you with suitable examples if you are asked to comment on your own company in an exam.

You will almost certainly be expected to know the SMART factors by heart, so learning them by rote is a good idea!

Without objectives there can be no strategy. Objectives determine the overall direction of the firm and also determine tactics since they are the guidelines by which junior managers make decisions. Each decision has to be made on the basis of whether it brings the firm (or the brand, or the department) nearer to achieving the stated objective.

CASE STUDY: J. Sainsbury PLC

This case study looks at the effects of objective setting in turning round a major corporation. The coordinating effects of setting appropriate objectives, derived from a clear vision, are illustrated.

Sainsbury's is one of the United Kingdom's largest grocery chains, with its beginnings in the mid-19th century. John James Sainsbury and his wife Mary opened their first store in London's Drury Lane, and by 1882 had four shops. Rapid expansion during the remainder of the century meant that by 1900 the firm had 48 shops, mainly in the London area.

Nowadays, the chain comprises 455 supermarkets and 301 convenience stores throughout the United Kingdom and employs 148,000 people. In October 2004, after losing ground substantially to other supermarket chains such as Tesco, the Sainsbury Board developed a recovery plan. Part of this plan was a restatement of the corporate vision, aimed at (in the Chairman's words) Making Sainsbury's Great Again (MSGA). The restated vision was as follows:

'We are here to serve customers well with a choice of great food at fair prices and, by so doing, to provide shareholders with strong, sustainable financial returns'.

This vision drove everything Sainsbury's did and thus was the coordinating force for the company. The recovery plan spanned 3 years, to March 2008, and involved making literally hundreds of changes, with major changes in product availability, updating the IT systems, better management of the supply chain and better price competition. Over the 3-year period, the company set the following key objectives:

1. To grow sales by £2.5 billion (excluding fuel sales). Groceries would contribute £1.4 billion of this, non-foods £700 million and convenience stores would contribute the rest.

2. To invest at least £400 million in improving product quality and price.

3. To find annual buying synergies equivalent to between 1 and 1.5%.

4. To generate cost efficiencies of at least £400 million.

5. To deliver neutral underlying cash flow for 2005/2006 and positive cash flow thereafter.

In the company's 2007 Annual Report, the Board reported the following achievements:

1. Sales had increased by £1 billion during 2006/2007, making a total increase of £1.8 billion over the first 2 years of the recovery plan – well on target.

2. The £400 million of investment was completed in December 2006 and additional investments had been made since.

3. The cost savings target was increased to £440 million, following the installation of new IT systems.

4. The underlying cash flow became positive in 2005/ 2006, somewhat early, so the objective for 2006/2007 was restated as achieving a neutral cash flow, allowing for substantial capital expenditures – this objective was also exceeded.

This success led Sainsbury's to establish a new 3-year plan, with an overlap with the existing plan: this plan would run until 2010 with the following objectives:

1. Growth of £3.5 billion in sales, split two-thirds food, one-third non-food.

2. Extend 75 stores to increase their selling area.

3. Continue to aim for supply chain efficiencies of 1–1.5% per annum, the savings to be invested in improving the customer offer.

4. Open 30 new supermarkets and 100 convenience stores.

5. Increase the number of stores offering home delivery from just over 100 to 200.

6. Make capital expenditures of £2.5 billion, funded from improved cash flow.

The company recognises that people are aiming to eat more healthily and also to eat more 'ethical' foods: the Sainsbury brand is well placed to meet these criteria, and the company expects to be able to build on their reputation for high-quality, healthy food rather than compete exclusively on price – at the same time, there is a recognition that there is a place for price competitiveness.

Overall, Sainsbury's are positioning themselves well for MSGA and fighting back against strong competition.

Questions

1. Why might Sainsbury's have revised the cost savings objective?

2. How do the objectives relate to the vision statement?

3. How might Sainsbury's management have arrived at the stated objectives?

4. How realistic is the new Sainsbury's 3-year plan?

According to McKay (1972) there are only three basic marketing objectives: to enlarge the market, to increase share of the existing market or to improve profitability within the existing market share. This somewhat simplistic view of objectives can be expanded to provide more concrete objectives: for example, enlarging the market can be carried out by bringing out new products aimed at a new group of customers, or by developing the existing products in order to reach new customers. These objectives can themselves be broken down further into developing existing end-use markets, or opening up new end-use markets. In each case, new objectives can be set.

In some cases, complexity in the problems facing the firm will lead to difficulties in setting objectives, because each possible solution to the problem simply creates another problem. Such complex problems are called wicked problems, because they have no definitive solutions.

ACTIVITY

The matrix below shows some current world problems. Place a tick in each box where you think the problems impinge on each other.

	Peace	Energy	Starvation	Civil rights	Population	Balance of payments
Peace						
Energy						
Starvation						
Civil rights						
Population						
Balance of payments						

Source: Mason, R. and Mitroff, I.: (1981) *Challenging Strategic Planning Assumptions*, New York: Wiley.

You should have few, if any, empty boxes at the end of this exercise. Now try putting the titles of typical business problems as the headings for the boxes. Usually you will find that the same thing happens – every problem impinges on every other, until there is no solution that will not result in a worsening situation somewhere else in the firm.

CASE STUDY: Procter and Gamble

This case study illustrates how strategy is developed and how a multinational is able to maintain flexibility across a wide range of markets by devolving strategic decision-making to local managers. It also illustrates some of the risks attached to making radical changes.

Procter and Gamble (P&G) owns what are among the world's best-known brands: Bold, Dreft, Pantene, Pringles, Sunny Delight and Febreze are among them. The company was founded in 1837 in Cincinnati, Ohio, by William Procter and James Gamble, a candle maker and a soap maker, respectively. The new company produced soap, washing powders and food products, but quickly diversified into producing a wide range of household goods, including foodstuffs.

In 1930 the company expanded by acquisition into the United Kingdom, buying out Thomas Hedley and Co., and in 1954 P&G established itself in Continental Europe. The company's commitment to developing new products and its commitment to staff development and promotion from within, led to P&G becoming one of the world's largest and most solid blue-chip companies, with a corporate culture to match.

At the beginning of 1999, however, P&G was facing something of a crisis. The bureaucracy had become overwhelming, the hierarchical organisation structure was threatening to slow down innovation and the sales were stagnating. The new chief executive, Durk Jager, vowed to take radical measures to turn the company round. A visionary leader, Jager wanted to transform P&G through his Organisation 2005 programme, a 6-year plan to improve sales and become a truly global (as opposed to multinational) company.

Organisation 2005 looked at re-organising the company around a matrix structure. Global business units (GBUs) were set up to oversee the various brand categories such as family care, skin care, hair care and feminine care. Coupled with this, the world was split up into market development organisations (MDOs) to implement brand strategies locally. Such a radical approach meant that virtually every senior manager changed jobs, systems throughout the company were overhauled and redesigned, and the corporate focus shifted away from the consumer and towards the internal business of who was doing what.

UK managing director Chris de Lapuente said of the changes, 'What we tried to do was change the whole organisation back to front, with a promise of record earnings. Virtually everybody changed jobs. And we were excited and inspired by the new vision and direction. It was very intoxicating. This was a winning culture and everybody signed up for it.' Unfortunately, the early promise of Organisation 2005 was not fulfilled – in fact, it was an almost total disaster.

Costs were slashed, but growth did not materialise and many loyal and experienced managers were alienated by the changes. Many middle managers departed, disillusioned by the arbitrary job shifts. The company lost sight of its customer focus and may have alienated some customers and damaged some brand values. Innovation dropped dramatically as development programmes were disrupted by the changes, and eventually Jager himself became a casualty of his own change programme.

The new CEO, A.G. Lafley, returned to basics and steadied down the rate of change. The rallying cry for P&G became, 'the consumer is boss', thus putting the consumer back at the core of everything the firm does. The implementation of this has been patchy, of course – de Lapuente himself says that targets are often expressed in terms of shareholder value or profit-and-loss rather than in market share terms. This in itself can cause conflicts.

The organisation structure has remained the same under Lafley as it was under Jager: GBUs have profit and loss responsibility on a global basis for the different categories they oversee. GBUs have broad responsibility for the vision, strategies and innovation in their own categories of brands, so they create marketing initiatives and templates which the MDOs then adapt for their local marketing programmes, geared to the local market wherever in the world they happen to be operating. This 'think global – act local' approach seems to be effective and de Lapuente believes that it is the way that all global companies will need to organise themselves in the long run – the potential rewards are outstanding. Overall objectives come from the top, with the CEO discussing with each of the GBU presidents the targets they will reach in terms of profits and shareholder value. MDO managers are then given the task of reaching those targets within their own regions. The fundamental measure for all the managers is shareholder value, but the focus might shift between focusing on profit and loss

and building market share – either of which will deliver shareholder value in the long run.

DeLapuente says that the similarities between the various global markets are much greater than the differences, which helps when trying to implement a global strategy on a local basis. P&G do not (in general) have local brands, so Pampers disposable nappies are the same product in every Western European country, as are Pringles crisps. There are exceptions – Daz washing powder is one example, since washing powders need to be adapted to suit local washing practices and washing machines, but in general brands are global. The fine-tuning of the strategy is evident in areas such as targeting for volume, for turnover, for market share, for running costs or for any of several other possible variables.

The key to balancing these different objectives is to be clear about which manager owns which part of the problem. 'If someone is saying their immediate priority is to drive the bottom-line profit, and someone else is saying no, we need to maximise volume, then you try and resolve that by moving to more "and" situations, in we want to maximise profit and volume,' DeLapuente says. What this means is that the marketing effort for the MDOs is geared towards implementation. This means devising the right marketing programmes: DeLapuente's MDO represents the second biggest market for P&G outside the United States and one which accounts for almost a quarter of all European sales. 'You can have the most wonderful strategies in the world', he says, 'but if the execution is flawed you have nothing'.

In the United Kingdom, the supermarkets have a stranglehold on food retailing, so dealing with individual customers requires a great deal of imagination and customisation. The supermarkets want things done their way – which means that the corporate strategy may need to be adapted considerably in practice. Price pressure from the supermarkets means that margins can be squeezed, which means there is less money available for innovation: this means that P&G now work closely with the retailers to develop compelling ideas to showcase P&G brands. DeLapuente believes that P&G are the market leaders in virtually every market they compete in, largely because of the corporate culture. The company promotes from within and is obsessed with winning; so many managers feel deeply upset if they are not winning. Interestingly, the company also places great emphasis on learning – people are encouraged to fail, in the sense that they are encouraged to take risks and failure is accepted as part of the price for innovation. Lessons learned are rapidly disseminated throughout the company.

Innovation is also the key to the company's creative approach to promotion. Although P&G do not ignore TV, they are involved in a wide range of activities, from providing educational materials for children, to hospital programmes for mothers with new babies, to sampling, to CD audio magazines, to interactive TV.

The results of the steadier approach to change management, and the commitment of P&G's employees and managers, are that the tide has now turned in the company's favour. For the fiscal year ended 2002 sales rose 3% overall to $40.2 billion, with net earnings up 49% to $4.4 billion. Ironically, industry experts believe that it may

have been the sharp shock administered by Organisation 2005 that reminded P&G of its fundamental strengths and brought the company back to concentrating on the customer.

Case study questions

1. What is the role of corporate culture in P&G's objective setting?

2. Why did the Organisation 2005 initiative fail?

3. What does the case study tell us about visionary leadership?

4. Why is P&G following a formal planning approach?

5. How might P&G resolve the inevitable conflicts between GBUs and MDOs?

Obviously, the vast majority of problems are 'tame' ones which have a fairly straightforward set of solutions. Only occasionally do managers have to tackle wicked problems, and they are usually solved at high levels in the organisation.

INTERNAL AND EXTERNAL INFLUENCES ON OBJECTIVES

Objectives cannot be set in a vacuum. Any manager needs to take account of the environment within which the firm operates. We have already seen that objectives that are perceived by staff as impossible or unrealistic will simply not be attempted, but equally an objective that does not take account of the realities of the external environment will not be achievable.

Internal influences include the following:

1. **Corporate culture.** This is the set of beliefs and behaviours shared by the members of the organisation. Corporate culture can only partly be influenced by management: typically it builds up from grass-roots level. Internal marketing has some role in developing an appropriate corporate culture.

2. **Resource constraints.** This is not only about money: resources also include staff knowledge and experience, and company assets such as patents, plant and equipment, premises and so forth. No company operates with infinite resources, so there will always be constraints and limitations, no matter how urgent or tempting the objective might be.

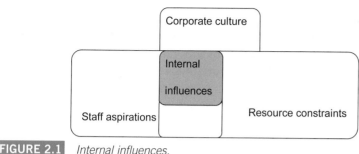

Internal influences.

3. **Aspirations of staff members.** Internal politics and career structures may affect the feasibility of corporate objectives. Employees primarily consider their own agendas – no one is going to damage his or her career simply to meet a corporate objective set by senior management.

As a general rule, staff members need to buy into any changes management tries to make to the corporate culture: in part, this is a problem for human resources departments (who may be able to recruit people who are already sympathetic to the culture) and in part it is a function of internal marketing, which will be covered in more detail in other modules (Figure 2.1).

MARKETING IN PRACTICE:
Aer Lingus

This example illustrates the importance of getting employees 'on side' and developing an appropriate corporate culture.

During late 1999, Aer Lingus ran a series of magazine advertisements in which they emphasised the friendliness of their staff. Much was said in the advertising about the warm welcome that Irish people traditionally give to strangers, but the most telling point was the headline: 'we don't spend money teaching people to smile at our customers. We just hire nice people to begin with'.

Although these advertisements were ostensibly aimed at the travelling public, their effect on the staff themselves was considerable. Aer Lingus staff (especially those with direct contact with passengers) felt rewarded for their efforts in being friendly to customers and felt encouraged to continue to do so: for an employee, the acknowledgement in the advertising was a clear indicator of expected behaviour. As a way of encouraging an appropriate corporate culture, as well as promoting a unique selling proposition in an industry which has few differentiators, the advertisements were a great success.

The Aer Lingus Marketing in Practice box demonstrates how a firm can develop an appropriate corporate culture by using a suitable recruitment policy.

External influences include the following:

1. **Competitors.** Any objective needs to take account of possible competitor responses, as well as current competitor behaviour. Competitors are not always predictable, but it is important to remember that they will always respond to any major changes in your own firm's marketing, so planners need to consider what possible retaliation might be in store and have responses ready. In some cases plans might be adapted or dropped altogether in order to minimise or negate competitive retaliation.

2. **Customers.** As in any question of marketing, objective setting should start with the customers. Knowing what customers want, knowing what they might want in future and knowing what they will find less interesting in future are of course crucial issues, but for objective setting it can be equally important to identify new groups of customers who might benefit from the company's product offerings.

3. **Government and legislation.** Objectives obviously need to be legal, but they should also be ethical, within the cultural context of the society in which the firm operates. For large firms, some objectives might provoke a Government response, even if the action is currently within the law.

4. **Technological advances.** This means more than just IT and communications – a technological advance could also mean a new drug on the market, a new way of making concrete, a new genetically modified crop or any number of other technical breakthroughs. The Marketing in Practice box about the Atkins diet illustrates a technical change which affected several industries.

MARKETING IN PRACTICE:
The Atkins Diet

This example illustrates how an environmental change – in this case a fashionable diet – can affect firms dramatically.

During 2003, the revolutionary Atkins diet suddenly became the 'diet of choice' of over 4 million British people. Despite warnings from some quarters that the diet was actually dangerous, its proven ability to help weight loss ensured its popularity among the large numbers of obese Britons raised on fish and chips and Mum's treacle pudding.

The Atkins diet advocates eating large amounts of protein foods and very little carbohydrate. Originally published in 1972, the diet received a tremendous publicity boost after actress Jennifer Aniston and former Spice Girl Victoria Beckham both claimed to have used it successfully. Meat sales grew by 11% and sales of some fruits (the ones allowed by Atkins such as watermelons and raspberries) also soared by as much as 64%. The Waitrose supermarket, mainly based in wealthy southern England, saw a 16% increase in meat sales, which a spokeswoman for the firm attributed to Atkins.

On the other hand, sales of bread and potatoes showed corresponding declines. The decline was steady – of the order of 1–2% per annum, but it was enough to have the bakers worrying. John White, the director of the Federation of Master Bakers, said, 'one can speculate as to the reasons, but personally I have no doubt that Atkins has had an impact. We can only hope that it's a fad that will pass'.

The Flour Advisory Bureau signed up model Denise van Outen to star in commercials promoting flour products. The British Potato Council spent £1 million on a makeover for the humble spud, and plans were laid for the potato, rice and flour industries to band together to meet the threat of Atkins.

Other diet products also felt the pinch. Roche's anti-obesity drug, Xenical, suffered a 16% drop in sales and Slim-Fast (a Unilever product) also showed a sharp decline. As 2004 started, however, some relief was on the horizon in the form of the South Beach Diet. Perhaps a new diet fad would replace Atkins in the public consciousness and save the carbohydrate industry.

Since 2004, the South Beach Diet has also gone the way of all fad diets, and although carbohydrates still have a bad name, people are beginning to realise that more exercise and less eating is probably the main way we have of losing weight. Dr. Atkins died in April 2003 from a head injury sustained when he slipped on an icy street: 2 years later his company filed for bankruptcy protection under the United States' Chapter 11 legislation. By that time less than 2% of Americans were on the Atkins diet, down from a peak of 11% in 2003. The global food industry may have breathed a sigh of relief – but sooner or later another dietary idea will come along!

The Marketing in Practice box on Benidorm shows how planning can go wrong, even when carried out carefully: a failure to recognise the consequences of short-termism, allowing any and all developments, is a major contributor to the failed dream. The planners also failed to take sufficient account of the market environment, which was rapidly changing as the Northern European economies became wealthy enough for most people to afford foreign holidays.

MARKETING IN PRACTICE: Benidorm

This example illustrates the potential problems which can arise even when everything is well-planned. External factors can easily disrupt the best-laid plans.

During the 1960s, town planners in Spain had the idea of creating a quiet respectable resort for the wealthier middle classes of Europe, foreseeing (correctly) that these people would have large disposable incomes and would be prepared to spend increasing amounts of their money on leisure, particularly as air travel became more widely available. The intended image of the resort was that of a peaceful town with an old quarter at its heart and upmarket, comfortable hotels around it.

The chosen area for the new resort was a small fishing village of 2,000 people, located about half an hour from the nearest airport, in an area with little in the way of natural resources apart from fairly constant sunshine all the year round. In 1958, the village mayor decided to hold a song contest to establish the town's reputation and to encourage the kind of respectable, middle-class arts lovers the town needed to feed its fledgling tourist trade and fill its hotels. The contest was a runaway success, mainly because the first contest spawned a major hit, over 70 versions of which were recorded worldwide. The resultant publicity would have put the town on the map even if the contest had never run again.

Unfortunately, although the publicity put the town on the map and started the developments rolling, the image of a quiet resort for the wealthy never materialised. The result of the careful planning was Benidorm – now widely regarded as the epitome of rampant overdevelopment and used as a byword for appalling resorts even by people who have never been there. The existing beach is excellent, but is now topped up with sand shipped in from the Sahara: acres of high-rise hotel and apartment development run for several miles along this seafront, and the original village is almost invisible. The original 2000 inhabitants have been supplanted by hotel workers, waiters, bar-owners and the like from all over Europe, and the resort is capable of coping with 5 million visitors a year. Maybe the original planners of Benidorm are not unhappy with the outcome – the town is nothing if not prosperous – but as a demonstration of the way things can turn out unexpectedly, Benidorm takes some beating!

ACTIVITY

Consider the internal and external environment of the firm you work for. What company objectives can you identify which are unpopular with staff? Which can you identify which are popular? What do you think will happen when these objectives are attempted?

What external factors might have led to these objectives being set in the first place?

Often objectives which are going to be unpopular with staff have come about because of overwhelming external issues. In some cases these external factors are not known to the staff concerned, which of course makes the introduction of unpopular policies incomprehensible.

ACTIVITY

Most people talk to their colleagues about work and where they think the organisation is going. Make a list of what you think are the shared beliefs of your company, based on conversations with your colleagues.

To what extent do these match with the 'official' beliefs stated in the corporate mission statement? How might you change the actual beliefs within the firm? Which beliefs would you need to change in order to improve the performance of the organisation?

CATEGORIES OF OBJECTIVES

Marketing objectives are usually derived from the wider corporate objectives. In the case of a truly marketing-orientated firm, corporate objectives and marketing objectives should be almost identical: but most firms are not as marketing orientated as this, by any means.

Corporate objectives are strategic statements of where the organisation's senior management thinks the organisation should be. Objectives can be grouped as follows:

- **Financial objectives.** These relate to sales, profits, return on investment, balance sheet issues and so forth.

- **Philosophical objectives.** These might encompass such factors as the core values of the organisation, a desire to be the biggest or the best or the most caring or (of course) customer orientation.

- **Qualitative objectives.** These are to do with service levels, the desire to be innovative or perhaps the desire to be respected as a good employer.

There will often be trade-offs in corporate objectives, since all organisations have limited resources and therefore cannot do everything they might want. The following is a list of possible conflicts in setting objectives (Weinberg, 1969):

1. **Short-term profit versus long-term growth.** Going for a quick profit is likely to sabotage longer-term steady growth, because the firm will launch products too soon, over-pressure customers to place orders now rather than later and cut back on long-term investments in research and brand building.

2. **Profit margin versus market positioning.** Investment in brand building and positioning the brand is likely to cost money, which of course affects the profit margin: likewise, some positions (e.g. a low-price position) will involve reducing margins so as to offer low prices.

3. **Direct sales effort versus market development.** Making quick sales may well involve tactics such as strong sales promotions which will affect people's perception of the brand in the longer term.

4. **Penetrating existing markets versus developing new ones.** Gaining greater sales from existing markets will take resources away from moving into new markets and vice versa. Penetrating existing markets is likely to require brand extensions or new products aimed at existing customers, whereas developing new markets (e.g. export markets) will require companies to promote heavily in those markets.

5. **Profit versus non-profit goals.** Almost all non-profit goals (e.g. becoming the best employer) will impinge badly on profit goals.

6. **Growth versus stability.** Following a growth strategy will inevitably result in disruptions within the firm as new management jobs are created and new responsibilities emerge. Stability has the advantage of being less risky, at least in the short term.

7. **Change versus stability.** As with growth, any other change will destabilise the company. On the other hand, firms which do not change in response to changes in their environment will eventually become obsolete.

8. **Low-risk versus high-risk environments.** Firms choosing a low-risk environment are likely to find that they earn relatively low returns: likewise firms in a high-risk environment may earn more if everything goes well, but could equally lose a great deal more if things go wrong.

Objectives will generate a set of sub-objectives in most cases: these are often tactical, which means that they can be changed relatively easily. Building up the strategic objectives by reaching the tactical objectives is the way in which firms progress.

Firms are not necessarily entirely profit maximising. Objectives may encompass many other outcomes (although firms will usually need to show a profit if they are to survive in the long term). The following are possible other objectives, but this list is not of course exhaustive.

- **Sales/revenue maximisation.** Firms may decide that maximising sales and revenue is a good way of shutting out competition and maintaining a strong presence in a competitive market. This may mean reducing profit: a firm which competes on price may sell more, but will certainly reduce profitability per unit sold and the extra sales may not compensate for this, so overall net profit may very well reduce.

- **Marketing objectives.** Some managers like to achieve high customer loyalty levels, or high levels of word-of-mouth recommendations. While these may not maximise profits, they do ensure survival: customer loyalty comes at a price, but does make the company more resistant to competitive pressure since loyal customers are (by definition) difficult to lure away. There are three generic marketing objectives: to increase market share, to increase profitability or to enlarge the existing market (McKay, 1972). Enlarging the existing market is usually only available to very large firms, and to be worthwhile the firm has to have a large enough share of the market not to have to worry about helping competitors (since competitors will gain from an overall enlargement).

- **Growth.** Often firms aim for growth rather than profit, since this again ensures survival. A growing firm will be investing more in marketing than one which is in a steady state, but the larger a firm is the less likely it is to have to go bankrupt if business drops off – it is relatively easy to find ways of cutting back.

- **Technological innovation.** Firms such as Sony and 3M pride themselves on their technical strengths. They are very much driven by engineering talent: in the case of Sony, the company was founded by two engineers and appears to exist mainly for engineers to enjoy creating novel electronic devices. Profit is simply a way of funding their inventiveness, rather than the other way round.

- **Ethical and social responsibility.** Body Shop is frequently quoted as a firm which has aimed for, and achieved, ethical trading as its prime objective. Fair Trade companies also exist purely as vehicles for social change and for whom profit is a necessary, but secondary, outcome.

As a general rule, most firms want to grow. This is for the following reasons:

1. **Protection against competition.** If the firm becomes one of the largest in the industry, competitors find it harder to enter the market. Growing firms are able to apply more resources to the market and take away market share from their competitors.

2. **Improved economies of scale.** Greater size means greater efficiency in almost everything: employees' time and skill is used more efficiently, the firm has greater purchasing power for raw materials and corporate resources (such as patents, designs and so forth) are used more intensively.

3. **Better control of the distribution networks.** A growing firm represents a more attractive proposition for suppliers and distributors because it is likely to generate more business for all concerned in the future. Growing firms thus have a negotiating advantage over others in the industry.

4. **More opportunities for career advancement.** Managers and employees of a growing firm have more opportunities for promotion, which means greater motivation and productivity. Also, having worked for a company which has grown is something which looks good on the managers' CV.

Growth is therefore a common aim, even if it is not quantified as an objective.

Clearly firms need to survive, but in most cases companies have many objectives other than profit maximisation. Sometimes these are enshrined in the company's mission statement. It is worth remembering that companies are run by people, each of whom has his or her own agenda, so in most cases profit is only a means to an end, not an end in itself.

In some cases, organisations are entirely non-profit-making. This does not preclude them from marketing, but it does mean that they may have multiple objectives and a wide range of 'customers' since they tend to manage exchanges with a wide range of stakeholders. This obviously complicates the marketing effort, since there may well be conflicts of interest between the stakeholders.

Typical objectives for non-profit organisations might be:

- **Charitable objectives** such as helping needy people or funding research into a disease. This would be a typical objective of a registered charity such as Oxfam or Médecins Sans Frontières.

- **Persuasive objectives** such as changing attitudes towards minority groups, promoting environmentalism or supporting a political party. Organisations such as Greenpeace, CND or the Labour Party fall into this category.

- **Financial objectives such as fund-raising.** This would be a typical objective for any non-profit group, since they all require a surplus of income over outgoings if they are to survive.

Sometimes non-profit organisations have a long-term survival need, but some may only exist for a short period to achieve a specific objective (e.g. lobbying Government for a single outcome such as preventing a hospital closure or raising money for an operation for a sick child).

USING THE MARKETING PLAN

The marketing plan, once it is in place, can be used in the following ways:

- **Delivering strategies and achieving objectives.** If the plan is well drawn, it should provide a clear blueprint for everyone in the firm. People should be able to know exactly what to do when they read the plan and (more importantly, perhaps) should know what everyone else is supposed to be doing.

- **Implement a marketing project.** The plan should help people make day-to-day decisions based on the overall direction of the plan. In other words, people should be able to make adjustments to the plan as circumstances dictate, without having to refer back to the senior managers.

- **Monitoring of progress.** The plan should contain enough information to enable staff to know whether they are meeting the objectives and staying on course to meet the overall strategic outcome. Corrections to the plan can be made in the light of new information: this may mean restating the objectives (see the Sainsbury's case study).

- **Managing implementation.** Staff should be aware of what needs to be done and when, and of course what other people will be doing and when. Deviations from plan should be obvious, and it should be straightforward for staff to make adjustments: clearly, someone will need to be in overall control, at least from a monitoring viewpoint, to remind people of target dates and deadlines.

- **Resource management.** The plan should enable managers to direct people, money and materials towards achieving the objectives. It should also enable planners to obtain resources which the organisation does not currently have.

- **Financial management.** The plan should enable long-term financial planning, in terms of both incoming revenues and outgoing expenditure.

- **Measurement of success.** The plan should enable managers to celebrate over-achievement or analyse under-achievement. Achieving objectives is satisfying and motivating for all concerned, which is another reason for ensuring that objectives are attainable: persistent failure to reach objectives is damaging to staff morale.

EXAM HINT

If you are asked to draw up a marketing plan, or even to outline some recommendations, be clear about exactly what you want people to do. You should also include monitoring and evaluation systems, with timescales, so that people can see what went wrong if the plan is not achieved. Remember that planning is one thing – achieving outcomes is another.

Many students lose marks by not making solid recommendations. You should be specific in what you are telling people to do – if you are asked for recommendations, say something that people can act on.

STAGES OF THE PLANNING PROCESS

Planning goes through distinct stages, as follows:

- **Corporate objectives are set.** These are the overall strategic objectives set by the directors of the firm. They may or may not be customer oriented, depending on the orientation of the firm, but almost all corporate objectives will rely on marketing to a greater or lesser extent. The corporate objectives may be very long term or relatively short term.

- **Marketing audit.** This is a snapshot of the company's current situation: there is more on this later in the module. Essentially, it covers everything the marketing managers need to know about the firm's internal and external environments, including competitors, customers, available resources and current activities and commitments. The marketing audit enables the planners to understand where the company is now, an important piece of information when deciding how to get to where we want to be.

- **Setting business and marketing objectives.** These objectives are set in terms of meeting the overall corporate objectives, so they might be seen as sub-objectives (i.e. tactical rather than strategic). This breaks down the overall objectives into manageable chunks for each department to handle.

- **Marketing strategies.** Strategy is about where we are going rather than about how we get there. Strategy is therefore concerned with determining where we should be as a firm and is usually (though not always) considered in terms of competitive position. The marketing strategy is aimed at meeting corporate objectives: in a completely market-oriented firm there will be little or no difference between corporate strategy and marketing strategy, but in most firms there is a distinction.

- **Marketing tactics/mix decisions.** Tactical decisions revolve around choosing the appropriate combination of marketing tools to achieve the overall strategic outcome. Tactical decisions are usually much easier to reverse or fine-tune than strategic decisions, since strategic decisions usually involve a lot of people doing diverse thing towards the strategy. There is more in Unit 3 about using the marketing mix to achieve tactical outcomes.

- **Implementation.** To an extent this is the moment of truth: putting the plan into action often reveals its flaws very quickly. Implementation is often carried out by more junior staff: it is helpful if they can be given the whole picture, in terms of the strategic plan, so that they are able to understand the purpose and intent of their part of it.

■ **Monitoring and control.** Having systems in place to check whether we are deviating from the plan is essential: having feedback systems which will allow us to make adjustments easily are also important. The systems should, ideally, enable managers to correct problems before they become too large.

THE MARKETING AUDIT

The marketing audit provides us with a quick overview of what the current situation is in terms of our marketing. The audit is shown in Table 2.1: you should note that this version of the audit is probably not exhaustive, but it does provide the main headings and can be used as a checklist.

Table 2.1	The marketing audit	
Main areas	**Subsections**	**Issues to be addressed**
Marketing environment audit		
Macro-environment	Economic–demographic	Inflation, materials supply and shortages, unemployment, credit availability, forecast trends in population structure.
	Technological	Changes in product and process technology, generic substitutes to replace products.
	Political–legal	Proposed laws, national and local government actions.
	Cultural	Attitude changes in the population as a whole, changes in lifestyles and values.
	Ecological	Cost and availability of natural resources, public concerns about pollution and conservation.
Task environment	Markets	Market size, growth, geographical distribution, profits; changes in market segment sizes and opportunities.
	Customers	Attitudes towards the company and competitors, decision-making processes, evolving needs and wants.
	Competitors	Objectives and strategies of competitors, identifying competitors, trends in future competition.
	Distribution and dealers	Main trade channels, efficiency levels of trade channels.
	Suppliers	Availability of key resources, trends in patterns of selling.
	Facilitators and marketing firms	Cost and availability of transport, finance and warehousing; effectiveness of advertising (and other) agencies.
	Publics	Opportunity areas, effectiveness of PR activities.
Marketing strategy audit	Business mission	Clear focus, attainability.
	Marketing objectives and goals	Corporate and marketing objectives clearly stated, appropriateness of marketing objectives.
	Strategy	Core marketing strategy, budgeting of resources, allocation of resources.
Marketing organisation audit	Formal structure	Seniority of marketing management, structure of responsibilities.
	Functional efficiency	Communications systems, product management systems, training of personnel.
	Interface efficiency	Connections between marketing and other business functions.
Marketing systems audit	Marketing information system	Accuracy and sufficiency of information, generation and use of market research.
	Marketing planning system	Effectiveness, forecasting, setting of targets.
	Marketing control system	Control procedures, periodic analysis of profitability and costs.
	New product development system	Gathering and screening of ideas, business analysis, pre-launch product and market testing.

Marketing productivity audit		
	Profitability analysis	Profitability of each product, market, territory and distribution channel. Entry and exit of segments.
	Cost-effectiveness analysis	Costs and benefits of marketing activities.
Marketing function audits		
	Products	Product portfolio; what to keep, what to drop, what to add, what to improve.
	Price	Pricing objectives, policies and strategies. Customer attitudes. Price promotions.
	Distribution	Adequacy of market coverage. Effectiveness of channel members. Switching channels.
	Advertising, sales promotion, PR	Suitability of objectives. Effectiveness of execution format. Method of determining the budget. Media selection. Staffing levels and abilities.
	Sales force	Adequate size to achieve objectives. Territory organisation. Remuneration methods and levels. Morale. Setting quotas and targets.

Source: Adapted from Kotler, P. (2003) *Marketing Management,* 11th edition, reprinted by permission of Pearson Education Inc., Upper Saddle River, NJ.

Basically, the audit is used to appraise the following aspects of the firm:

- **The internal and external environment.** This means determining what resources we have at our disposal and what is out there in the external environment for us to deal with.

- **Organisational SWOT.** This is necessary but not sufficient: SWOT analysis is only the beginning of the process and is in any case a subjective and inaccurate tool.

- **Organisational competencies and capabilities.** This is about what are able to do, in terms of our skills and internal resources: SWOT analysis looks at our strongest capabilities, but we also need to consider everything that we can do competently. We do not have to be the best at everything to be able to do things competently, in other words.

- **Organisational resource versus capacity to deliver.** Our resources are a large part of our capacity to do what we say we are going to do – although the effectiveness with which we use those resources is also crucial. The main issue here is that we should not promise anything we cannot deliver, since this destroys good will and creates negative word of mouth.

- **Competitor analysis.** We always need to remember that our competitors are not standing still. They have their own plans which will affect us, and they are very likely to respond to anything we do, especially, if it threatens their own plans.

The audit does have some 'health warnings' attached to it. First, it only provides a snapshot: by the time the full audit has been carried out, the situation may well have changed anyway, so it only provides a backward view. Second, it is not an objective tool. It does require judgement and even guesswork. Third, it will not make the decisions for you – it is only a way of generating and organising information, and to an extent focusing on the managers' thinking.

Having said all that, the audit is an excellent starting point for objective setting and also (if carried out regularly) a good way to monitor progress. It also has the major advantage of focusing management thinking – conscientiously carried out, the marketing audit provides managers with an unrivalled opportunity to consider every aspect of the firm's situation before making decisions.

3. Which of the following is true?

   A Aspirations of staff members are part of the external environment.

   B Corporate culture is dependent on staff 'buying in'.

   C Resource constraints are irrelevant to the internal environment.

4. Technological breakthroughs are examples of:

   A External influences.

   B Resource constraints.

   C Competitive forces.

5. Which of the following is true?

   A Corporate objectives come before the marketing audit but after setting the objectives.

   B Objectives are set after the marketing audit but before the marketing strategies are decided.

   C Marketing strategies are set before the objectives and after the marketing audit.

FURTHER READING

Chapter 10 of *Essentials of Marketing* (Blythe). Alternatively, Chapters 2 and 10 of *Principles of Marketing* (Blythe), Chapter 21 of *Principles of Marketing* (Brassington and Pettitt), Chapter 3 of *Principles of Marketing* (Kotler et al.) and Chapter 2 of *Principles and Practice of Marketing* (Jobber).

JOURNAL ARTICLES

Chimhanzi, J. (2004): The impact of integration mechanisms on marketing/HR dynamics, *Journal of Marketing Management*, **20**(7/8), September: 713–740.

Porter, M.E. (1990): How competitive forces shape strategy, *Harvard Business Review* **57**(2) 137–145.

WEBSITES

http://www.businessballs.com/freebusinessplansandmarketingtemplates.htm
This site gives advice and a template for planning.

http://www.websitemarketingplan.com/marketing_plan2.htm
This website offers a wide range of articles on improving your marketing
   planning.

http://www.bplans.co.uk/sample_plans/marketingplans.cfm
This site has a large number of templates for all kinds of businesses:
   unfortunately, it is American, which means that the plans would need
   considerable adaptation, but they do offer 'worked examples'.

REFERENCE

McKay, E.S. (1972) *The Marketing Mystique*, New York: American Management
   Association.

CHAPTER 3

The Marketing Mix

Learning objectives

After working through this section, and carrying out the associated reading, you should be able to:

- Explain the principles of product planning.
- Explain the product life cycle.
- Explain the importance of introducing new products and services.
- Explain the new product development (NPD) process.
- Explain the effect of price on the other elements of the marketing mix.
- Describe the different pricing methods.
- Define the different components of distribution channels and show how they work together to create a distribution strategy.
- Explain the factors that influence channel and distribution decisions.
- Evaluate the range of marketing communication tools and consider their usefulness in different circumstances.
- Evaluate the range of communications media and consider their impact in different circumstances.
- Explain the contribution of people, process and physical evidence to the marketing mix.
- Describe the different methods for measuring marketing outcomes.
- Explain the adoption of services and products in terms of customer characteristics.
- Show how a coordinated marketing mix contributes to customer satisfaction and competitive advantage.

The marketing mix is the basic set of tools marketers have available to carry out tactical marketing. The mix is generally thought of as being like the ingredients in a recipe – they need to be combined in the correct proportions and at the correct time if the overall result is to be a success. As in a recipe, one ingredient cannot substitute for another – they all work together to produce a result. The proportions of the mix necessarily need to be different according to the product type, corporate resources and of course the consumers' characteristics.

The basic mix elements were originally thought to be as follows:

1. **Product.** This is the bundle of benefits the firm offers to the customer, and is the element which is intended to meet people's needs. The product is not necessarily physical – it could be a service, and indeed most products contain elements of both service and physical

2. **Price.** This is the total of what the firm expects the customer to do in return. Price goes beyond the amount the company receives – it also includes other costs the consumer has to pay, such as the cost of learning to use the product, the cost of switching from their existing product, the cost of installation and so forth.

3. **Place.** This is the location where the exchange takes place – the retail store, through the mail, in cyberspace, etc. Place decisions involve thinking about physical distribution (shipping and delivery) as well as about finding the most convenient location for customers to buy the product.

4. **Promotion.** This is the subgroup of mix elements which the marketer uses to communicate the total offer to the customer. Promotion is itself divided into a promotional mix, and new ways of communicating are being added almost daily.

This categorisation of mix elements proved to be inadequate, since it has only limited application to service products: since services now comprise the bulk of marketing in the developed world, extra mix elements need to be considered. They are as follows:

5. **People.** These are the 'front-line' staff who deliver the service benefits to the customer, for example, the chef, waiters and waitresses in restaurants or the legal personnel in a law firm. For the customer, these people are perceived as the suppliers: their attitudes, behaviour and skill are the products the customer is buying.

6. **Process.** This is the system by which the product benefits are delivered. A self-service restaurant differs in process from an a la carte restaurant, for example. Process not only defines part of the product, but also has implications for the cost base of the supplying company. In many businesses, ordering online has streamlined the purchase process, and many service companies operate online booking systems (airlines, hotels, some restaurants, ferry companies and so forth).

7. **Physical evidence.** This is the tangible aspect of the service delivery. The décor, the tablecloths, the menus and so forth in a restaurant are all evidence of the service being delivered: in some services such as insurance, glossy brochures or imposing office buildings provide physical evidence. From a consumer's viewpoint, physical evidence is useful in judging the expected quality of the service provision.

EXAM HINT

If you are asked to discuss the marketing mix of a service business, remember that you are being asked for all seven elements, not just the last three. You will definitely lose marks if you do not discuss product, price, place and promotion if asked to comment on the marketing of, say, a retail store.

You should also remember that the product consists of the benefits the retailer supplies – this is not necessarily the same as the physical products they sell. In other words, what the retailer supplies is convenience, a pleasant in-store atmosphere, reassurance of quality and perhaps even some prestige if the retailer is an upmarket one.

Finally, almost all products have both a service element and a physical element – the 7P model covers all products, therefore, not just those which we normally define as 'service' products.

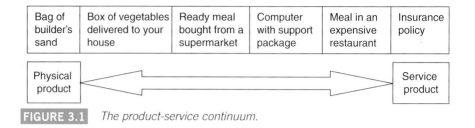

FIGURE 3.1 *The product-service continuum.*

Many academics regard the distinction between physical products and service products as artificial, since most products contain elements of both: generally speaking, current thinking is that all products are somewhere on a continuum between physical and service elements, with some products containing a higher service element than others. Having said that, if a product is close to the 'service' end of the spectrum, the marketing mix will emphasise different elements more than would be the case for a product near the 'physical' end of the spectrum, and consumer behaviour will be different in each case.

In Figure 3.1, an insurance policy represents an entirely service-based product. There is no physical existence at all (apart from the policy document, which has no intrinsic value except as physical evidence). A meal in an expensive restaurant is mainly composed of the service element – the waiters, the chefs, the ambience, etc. – but there is a physical element in that there is actually some food. A computer with a support package is much more of a physical product, but the support service may represent quite a large proportion of the price and could be a very large proportion of the value the consumer gets from the product. A ready meal bought in a supermarket has some service element (since it has been prepared by someone and is offered for sale in a retail outlet) but is mainly a physical product. A box of vegetables is almost entirely physical – only the delivery element is a service. Finally, a bag of building sand is entirely physical, with no discernible service element.

STUDY TIP

Although the elements of the marketing mix need to be learned individually, each element impinges on every other element. In practice, you cannot consider the elements in isolation, so you need to cultivate the habit of thinking how an adjustment to one element will affect all the other elements.

In particular, many of the elements overlap – price, for example, conveys an impression of quality, which is part of the product benefit and also part of the promotional mix. Likewise promotion might be considered as part of the product: owning a well-known and well-regarded brand (such as Nike or Rolex) conveys very real benefits to the customer.

We will now look at each of the elements individually. Always keep in mind that the elements of the promotional mix do not operate in isolation – each one affects the others, in the same way as each ingredient in a recipe affects the flavour or texture of every other ingredient.

EXAM HINT

Whenever you are asked to consider changes to one element of the promotional mix, you should try to think about how the other elements will be affected: you will gain marks if you can explain these effects and come up with answers for how to handle such changes.

PRODUCT

A product is a bundle of benefits. From a customer's viewpoint, it is the benefits that are important: we, as consumers, are only interested in how the product will improve our lives, not in what it is made of, where it came from, how it was developed or anything else about it. If we do not believe that the product will improve our lives, no amount of persuasion will change our minds.

ACTIVITY

Thinking about the organisation you work for, make a list of the benefits your products provide to the people who buy them. This is easy if you work for a manufacturer or a service business like a restaurant or pizza delivery company – but not so easy if you work for a training company or a charity.

If you work for a non-profit organisation like a charity, you need to define who your customers are. If you answer that it is the beneficiaries of the charity, you would need to explain what they are providing to you as their part of the exchange – so maybe it is the people who give money to the cause who are the real customers. In that case, what benefits are you providing for them? What might you do to add value, so that they are more likely to give to your charity rather than another one?

Whatever your organisation, you need to provide benefits if you are to receive money. The next problem would be to work out what features the product must have if it is to provide the benefits you have identified.

Competitors continually offer new products, and at the same time our own products become outdated, old-fashioned and (eventually) obsolete. Therefore, developing new products becomes extremely important for any firm, since companies must offer something different from competing products if they are to win customers. Products can be studied at different levels, as explained by Levitt (1986) when he outlined the total product concept.

The basic core product is what is offered by all companies in the market – for example, a car will carry the driver, his or her luggage and passengers, and take them from one place to another via the road system. All cars provide these benefits as a minimum: this is the *core* or *generic* product. Moving beyond this is the *expected* product, which is the core product plus features that the average person would reasonably expect to see. In the car example, people would expect the car to have a radio, a heater, windscreen wipers and so forth. Few cars would lack these basic features (although there was a time when windscreens were an optional extra, and even quite recently radios were not standard in cars). The *augmented* product includes features and benefits which distinguish the product from its competitors: for example, the car might have an automatic engine cut-out when the car is stationary or might have windscreen wipers which sense when it is raining. Finally, the *potential* product has all the features and benefits anyone could want or need. In fact, no products fit into that category because there are so many potential needs – and it would probably be unwise to try to offer such a product to the market, since the cost would be prohibitive.

Elements of the product include the following:

- **Branding.** The brand is the 'personality' of the product, conveying important information about the expected quality, the expected performance and the reaction we might expect from our friends if they know we have bought the product. This last factor is by no means unimportant – people often define themselves by the brands they buy. The brand is, in effect, the 'lens' through which the customers see the product and through which the marketers project their offerings.

- **Product lines and product ranges.** Marketers need to manage a portfolio of products: very few firms market only one product. The portfolio may be broad (a wide range of product categories) or deep (a range of variations on a product designed to reach all of a target market). Sometimes products need to be dropped from the range, not because they are unprofitable, but because the resources they take up can be better employed elsewhere. Portfolio management is an important part of marketing, as is NPD.

- **Packaging.** The design of the packaging often renders products more desirable, more noticeable on the retailers' shelves and more informative in terms of product benefits. At its most basic, packaging protects the product from the environment and vice versa. Marketers also need to consider customer use of packaging and the environmental impact of different packaging options. For example, a gardener might use empty plastic soft drink bottles to protect seedlings, or someone might use old coffee jars to store small items such as screws or nails. In some cases, packaging has become the differentiating factor for the product – some fast-food delivery services use reusable plastic containers, while others use disposable foil ones:

clearly the plastic ones are more useful, and this might be the deciding factor between choosing one takeaway outlet over another. Disposal of used packaging has, of course, become a hot topic in recent years due to its environmental impact.

- **Service support.** Many physical products have a service element, if only in terms of after-sales service or customer support helplines. This is especially true in business-to-business markets, which represent the bulk of marketing activity, far outweighing business-to-consumer marketing. Service support can often be the only differentiator a firm can offer, when rival products are similar or even identical. For example, engine oil must be similar or identical in its formula to all other engine oils, since the engine manufacturer will have designed the engine specifically to use a particular grade of oil. Oil companies cannot make major changes to the physical product, so they need to compete on service support, for example, by offering technical advice to motor mechanics or by making the product available in more convenient retail outlets.

CASE STUDY: HJ Heinz

It has been many years since Heinz had only 57 varieties. In fact, the number 57 was chosen by the company's founder, Henry J. Heinz, simply because he liked the sound of it – it had no other significance.

HJ Heinz produces almost 6,000 varieties, spread across 200 brands worldwide. Food is produced and sold in eight different categories: convenience meals, condiments and sauces, infant feeding, weight control, frozen food, pet food, foodservice and seafood. Although the parent company is American, the British part of the company is the biggest overseas subsidiary, and many British consumers think of the company as British.

Managing such a huge range of products is by no means simple. In the United Kingdom, the Jones Knowles Ritchie packaging design company took over the account in 1997 and found a wide range of different packaging designs in place. The situation had grown up because each product had its own particular packaging problems and needs – but the situation had got out of hand, with no clear brand image being presented and a confusing message being presented to consumers.

Meanwhile, Heinz USA had decided to follow the example of its Weightwatchers brand and lose some weight. The company sold off its pet food business in 2002 and a number of its other marginal brands over the next few years. In the United Kingdom, sales of salad cream were falling – salad cream is an entirely British product, with virtually no market outside the United Kingdom. Also, healthy eating was becoming the latest fad – demand for organic food, low-fat food and even low-carb food as a result of the popularity of the Atkins Diet meant that Heinz had to make a number of tough decisions.

Jones Knowles Ritchie began by linking all the different products through the Heinz Keystone design – the badge-shaped symbol which appears on all Heinz products. The agency realised that what consumers thought was important was the quality symbolised by the Heinz brand, rather than the actual product contained in the bottle or can. This still left plenty of scope for individualising the brands – the turquoise colour used for the baked beans (reputedly because it enhances the colour of the beans when the can is opened) could remain, as well as the individual graphics for the children's products such as Eazy Squirt.

Heinz' PR consultants issued a statement that salad cream might be withdrawn due to falling sales. This press release made the TV news, and amid a flurry of protests from millions of Britons who had grown up with salad cream, the threat was withdrawn. Sales rose sufficiently for Heinz to introduce an organic version of salad cream, to be sold alongside its existing traditional salad cream as well as the ever-expanding range of organic products. In February 2003, the Soil Association (Britain's leading promoters of organic food) gave Heinz an award for their organic range of foods.

In the United States, Heinz introduced 'one-carb' sauces which are low-carbohydrate sauces intended for Atkins dieters.

Managing the portfolio is, for Heinz, a constant, dynamic process. Introducing new products to meet consumer needs, cutting out products which no longer show sufficient profit, packaging products in an eye-catching manner, and responding to the rapidly changing world of nutrition are continual activities for Heinz managers. This may be why Heinz has such a solid place in the hearts and minds of consumers.

Questions

1. Why might Heinz drop its pet foods range, when the products were still making money for the firm?
2. What is the importance of packaging to Heinz?
3. How has the Heinz brand developed across the range?
4. What other changes might Heinz introduce to coordinate the branding better?
5. Why might the company subdivide its brands into eight categories?

ACTIVITY

Find data on your company's product range, if possible going back 20 years. Which products are still available from 20 years ago? Which were viable products 20 years ago, but are now no longer offered? Why were these products dropped?

Which recently introduced products do you expect will still be around 20 years from now?

(If you work for an organisation which has not been around for 20 years, you could look at the industry as whole for this period.)

THE PRODUCT LIFE CYCLE

The product life cycle is an important concept for marketers. Basically, the model states that products go through a series of stages, as follows. Each of these stages will be discussed in more depth later (Figure 3.2).

1. **Development.** Products do not arrive fully formed: managers, marketers, engineers, designers and researchers need to consider product ideas and turn them into viable, feasible, profitable products. There is more on the development process later.

2. **Introduction.** The product is launched onto the market: at first, it is likely to lose money, because the cost of developing and marketing it has not yet been recovered and sales are likely to be small at first. In many cases, products do not move on from this stage, and in fact the

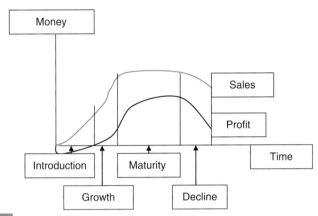

FIGURE 3.2   *The product life cycle.*

majority of new products fail. The losses they make have to be covered by the products which do go on to succeed.

3. **Growth.** If the product is accepted by consumers, sales will rise and so will profits, although during the growth phase the product will still need considerable marketing expenditure. The growth stage can be problematic, since at any point a competing product may enter the market or some other change may occur which curtails the growth.

4. **Maturity.** Sales will eventually level off, at which point the product is established in the market and will need less support: at this point, profits will be high, and the company will start to get a real return on the investment. In the maturity phase, the company will still need to promote the product (using 'reminder' campaigns) in order to fend off competitors.

5. **Decline.** Sales will eventually fall off as competitors enter the market, or as consumer tastes and preferences change. During the decline phase, the product will probably still be profitable: at this point, marketers may decide to develop a 'Mark Two' version of the product or alternatively remove all support and let the product die.

6. **Obsoletion.** Finally, the product will become obsolete and be withdrawn or at least dramatically downgraded. Sometimes profit can still be made from such products, since they require virtually no investment in marketing: sometimes these products can be re-launched in new markets, and in fact this was a popular tactic in the motor industry during the 1970s, when Western European car manufacturers sold obsolete designs and machine tool patterns to Eastern European manufacturers. For a while, Polish and Russian versions of Fiat designs were re-imported into the West at extremely low prices.

The product life cycle is not necessarily followed by all products. Some will have regular revivals (children's toys such as the Hula hoop and the yo-yo are often used as examples), while others never really get off the starting blocks and disappear within a short time of being introduced. Others may fail initially, but be repositioned into another market and find success elsewhere. Another problem with the PLC is that outcomes are not measurable or predictable – there is really no way of knowing whether the product has reached maturity, or how long the maturity stage will last, or how long the decline phase will be or how steep the decline curve, since we have no way of predicting when a competitive response might prove too strong for the product.

The main usefulness of the PLC as a concept, and the reason it is still widely taught, is that it highlights the reason for developing new products. The PLC concept tells us that (eventually) all products will become obsolete and will disappear: a company which does not develop new products to replace those which go out of fashion or are superseded by competitors will eventually itself disappear.

CASE STUDY: Smith and Nephew

In 1856, a pharmaceutical chemist named Thomas James Smith opened a shop in Hull, UK. Forty years later, his nephew Horatio Nelson Smith became his business partner, and the firm of Smith and Nephew was created. Horatio was interested in developing dressings for wounds, and the business moved towards the manufacture of bandages and other dressings.

Massive expansion during the First World War (to meet the needs of wounded soldiers) took the company from 50 employees to 1,200 in only 4 years. In 1928, the company began development of Elastoplast, the adhesive bandage designed to compete with Johnson & Johnson's recently introduced Band-Aid bandage. Band-Aid and Elastoplast were, at the time, revolutionary products: Band-Aid, introduced in 1920, only sold $3,000 worth in its first year and was hand-made until 1924. Elastoplast was originally a cloth bandage with an antiseptic pad and adhesive edges: it was not until 1966 that the company introduced the Airstrip variant, which was a ventilated plastic adhesive strip with an antiseptic pad.

Smith and Nephew expanded by acquisition during the 1970s and 1980s, in the process of which the company acquired subsidiaries which produced medical equipment such as orthopaedic implants and continuous passive motion machines, which keep patients' joints moving after surgery in order to avoid stiffness. Smith and Nephew were thus beginning to move away from their concentration on wound management and heading into general areas of patient recovery.

This in turn led to an interest in surgery. Smith and Nephew have been at the forefront of developing endoscopy – the so-called keyhole surgery – which enables surgeons to use an extremely small incision when carrying out internal surgical procedures. Endoscopy uses miniature cameras and remote surgical instruments, and is being used more and more widely as surgeons realise the benefits of causing the minimum wound. Patients can often leave hospital the same day as their surgery and recovery times are markedly faster.

In 1999, Smith and Nephew bought out 3M's shoulder and hip implant business: the company also announced a new three-part Group Strategy, focused on orthopaedics, endoscopy and wound management. During 2000, this new strategy led the company to sell off its feminine hygiene and its toiletries products in a management buyout. Elastoplast was sold to Beiersdorf AG, who also took over the distribution of Nivea in the United Kingdom. Thus Smith and Nephew pulled out of the consumer products market entirely, concentrating solely on its products for health care professionals. The company now offers over 1,000 products and continually spends on research and development to increase the range and efficacy of its products. During 2003, the company spent £67 million in R&D – 6% of the company's total turnover. Research is concentrated in the company's three strategic areas.

Graphic proof of the efficacy of Smith and Nephew's products came in October 2002. The Bali bombing killed over 200 people, but the wounds suffered by other victims were truly horrific. One young mother of two suffered 85% burns: she was treated immediately with Smith and Nephew's Acticoat dressing, and in the Sydney hospital where she was taken she was treated with Transcyte temporary skin until skin grafts could be carried out. Even 5 years earlier, a patient with 85% burns would not be expected to live – but this mother was discharged from hospital within a month and was able to spend Christmas with her children.

Case study questions

1. Why would Smith and Nephew sell off its consumer products divisions?

2. Why does the company spend such a large portion of its turnover on research?

3. What stage of the PLC was Band-Aid in during 1924?

4. What stage of the PLC was Elastoplast in when Smith and Nephew sold it?

5. To what extent are Smith and Nephew's products customer specified?

PORTFOLIO MANAGEMENT

Very few companies produce only one product. This means that most marketing managers have to deal with several products within a range, each at a different stage of the product life cycle and each with its own group of customers. Some products will be at the beginning of the life cycle, others will be in the growth or maturity stages and still others will be in decline: managers need to make decisions on what to do about each product in terms of marketing it.

Probably, the best-known portfolio management tool is the Boston Consulting Group Matrix (see Figure 3.3). This categorises products according to their market share and the growth rate of the market they are in. The categories are as follows:

1. A Star is a product with a large share of a growing market. This product will grow in sales and profits, but will need to be protected from incoming competitors, so may need a lot of marketing support.

2. A Problem Child is a product with a small share of a growing market. This product is problematic because it will need a lot of effort to grow its market share, but if this can be done it has the potential to become a Star. If, on the other hand, the effort fails, then a lot of investment of time and money will have been wasted, and it would have been better simply to drop the product from the range.

3. A Cash Cow is a product which has a large share of a stable market. It is probably in the maturity stage of the PLC and probably needs relatively little marketing input to maintain its position: this means that it will continue to generate income for the firm over a long period of time.

		Relative market share	
		High	Low
Market growth	High	Star	Problem Child
	Low	Cash Cow	Dog
	Negative	War horse	Dodo

FIGURE 3.3 *The expanded BCG matrix.*

4. A Dog is a product which has a small share of a stable market. Dogs are not likely to be profitable and are prime candidates to be dropped from the range: however, in some cases Dogs are kept on, perhaps because they have a historical significance to the company, perhaps because sales of other products depend on them, or perhaps because some loyal customers might defect if the Dog were dropped. In any case, they require little expenditure and therefore can be 'harvested' for their remaining income.

Researchers called Barksdale and Harris later added two more categories to the list, to reflect the possibility that a market might actually be shrinking, as follows:

5. A Warhorse is a product with a large share of a shrinking market. Like the Cash Cow, it is probably profitable and will certainly require very little support, since a shrinking market is probably not of interest to competitors, so it can provide good cash returns, at least in the short term.

6. A Dodo is a product which has a small share of a shrinking market. It is extremely unlikely to be worth keeping and will in any case eventually disappear along with its market. An example might be a product which is kept on for historical or sentimental reasons (perhaps because it has an aging, but loyal, customer group).

The BCG Matrix and its variants certainly provide a good way of focusing the mind on product portfolio management, but it suffers from the major drawback that it is subjective. Deciding what is a large (or small) share is a managerial judgement, nothing to do with any objective criteria, and it may be hard to judge whether a market is growing, shrinking or stable at any one time.

Having decided that a product is at a particular point on the PLC, and in the BCG Matrix, managers then need to decide what to do about it. Promotion policy, distribution policy and pricing policy all are affected by this estimation. Most importantly, though, is the NPD policy.

ACTIVITY

List all the products your organisation offers. Now try to categorise them as Cash Cows, Stars, Dogs and so forth. Can you explain why the company does not simply drop Dogs and Dodos? How did you decide that those products ARE Dogs and Dodos?

Would you be able to justify your position to your boss?

NEW PRODUCT DEVELOPMENT

There are three main reasons for introducing new products and services:

1. **Changing customer needs.** As time moves on, customers change their requirements, and new generations of consumers appear bringing with them different ideas and needs.

2. **Technological changes.** Changes in communications technology mean that many services (such as travel agencies) have been severely hit by online services. At the same time, the Internet and other communications systems (such as mobile telephones and texting) have opened up new opportunities for services which could not have existed even 10 years ago. Technological change is not confined to communications and electronics, of course: a new method of making concrete could have profound effects on the construction industry, and a new diet discovery can disrupt the food industry dramatically.

3. **Long-term business strategies.** New products can often put the company into new competitive positions, perhaps even against new competitors. For example, a motor manufacturer's decision to expand in the Third World might mean developing an easily maintained, reliable, cheap basic vehicle for use on poor roads in remote areas.

NPD follows a series of stages in most cases (Figure 3.4). These are as follows:

1. **Idea generation.** Ideas might come from any source – customers, staff, research and development officers, senior management and so forth. Some companies have dedicated teams of people charged with

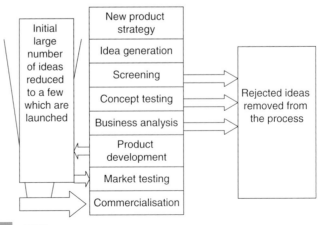

FIGURE 3.4 *NPD process.*

the task of thinking of new ideas: such groups are often drawn from several different departments in order to take advantage of different experience, specialist knowledge and different perspectives.

2. **Screening.** Ideas are discussed, and the most promising ones put forward for further development. Screening should only take place once all the ideas (however far-fetched) have been assembled. Trying to screen ideas as they are formulated tends to make people self-conscious and reluctant to offer their thoughts and also tends to impede discussion within the group. Even the worst idea might trigger a better one or be combined with a later idea to create a successful product.

3. **Concept testing.** The basic idea behind each product is shown to potential customers and their comments are invited. Sometimes this can be done via formal market research; in other cases, it might simply involve informal discussions with potential customers. At this stage, there is unlikely to be any kind of prototype or mock-up: people are only being asked to comment on the basic idea.

4. **Business analysis.** The degree to which the product will fit with existing products and with existing corporate strategies is assessed. Products which might harm existing sales, or which take the company in undesirable directions, will be dropped at this stage. Profitability (or at least the degree of fit with the corporate mission) will be considered at this stage, although it is unlikely that a definitive assessment can be undertaken since the costs of developing the product and manufacturing it will not be known until the engineers have carried out their part of the process.

5. **Product development.** Once the business analysis shows that the product should be viable, the actual engineering process can begin. Prototypes will be produced and tested, and engineering problems will be overcome: feedback from the market will need to be considered, and competitors' products might also be tested as part of the process. Sometimes competing products are 'reverse engineered', meaning that company engineers will dismantle the competing product to find out how it has been made.

6. **Market testing.** Often, though by no means always, the product will be offered to a section of the market in order to test its potential sales. This enables the company to assess the potential for the product before committing fully to it, with all the marketing and production costs entailed. In other cases, individuals might be asked to use the product and report on it: for example, a new type of house paint might

be offered to several hundred people to try out, and these people might later be interviewed to find out how they found the product. The drawback of market testing is that competitors may find out about the product and prepare their retaliation before the product is established.

7. **Commercialisation and launch.** Finally, the product is launched to the full market. At this point, there should be a complete marketing plan and a full commitment by the company. Even so, the majority of new products fail to recoup their development costs – there are simply too many variables for NPD to be an exact science.

Usually, these stages would be followed in the order given, but occasionally stages might be skipped or might be carried out in another sequence. In some cases, especially in volatile industries such as consumer electronics, several stages might be carried out in parallel – for example, concept testing, business analysis and even product development might overlap. In other industries, the whole process might be dramatically shortened or bypassed. For example, a restaurant might simply put a new recipe on the 'Daily Specials' board, offer it to the lunchtime customers and gauge their reaction to it. If the response is generally negative, the dish can be omitted in future, but a positive response might lead to it being added to the main menu.

EXAM TIP

You will certainly be expected to consider the circumstances of the company if you are asked to outline the NPD process for a case study. A pharmaceutical company might have a huge research budget with extremely long lead times – 10 or 15 years – for developing new products, while a small light engineering company might simply be told what to make by a large customer, with no real development process at all.

If you think a company will not follow the full process for some reason, simply say so in your answer and outline what you think should happen. This will show that you understand the NPD process, but can use some common sense when applying it.

CASE STUDY: Gillette

When King C. Gillette was 40, he was working as a sales representative for Crown Cork and Seal Company of Wisconsin. He was making a good living, but the job required a smart turn-out, including being clean-shaven. One morning he noticed that his cut-throat razor was blunt and was in fact so worn out that it would not take an edge and could therefore not be sharpened. At that point he had the flash of inspiration that has changed the world for men – he had the idea of producing a disposable blade that would simply be thrown away when it became blunt.

After some years of experimenting, he found a way to make the blades and also found a machine tool which could stamp out and sharpen the blades. Unfortunately, the cost of making the blades was higher than the price he could get for them – so this was where his sales training paid off.

Gillette realised that he could only get the production costs down if he produced blades in the millions, which meant converting a lot of men to the idea of using a disposable blade. At first, he sold the blades below cost to build up the business, but this was too slow. Then he hit on a business idea which is still used in the 21st century. He gave away the razors which held the blades in place and made his money selling the blades. Millions of the razors were handed out free, so millions of men tried the new system, and having done so very few went back to the old cut-throat razors.

By the time he was 55, Gillette was a millionaire, and the cut-throat razor was a thing of the past. Nowadays, the company he founded is a worldwide organisation, marketing items as diverse as toothbrushes and Duracell batteries.

Gillette have a history of being first to market. Following on from the launch of the world's first safety razor in 1901, the company went on to launch the following new products:

- twin-bladed razor, 1972
- twin-bladed disposable razor, 1976
- pivoting head razor, 1979
- pivoting head disposable razor, 1980
- razor designed specifically for women – Sensor, 1992
- triple blade razor – Mach 3, 1998

Note that the rate of innovation increased rapidly after 1970. For 70 years, the company had produced essentially the same product: competition had been held off at first by King C. Gillette's original patents, but eventually competitors entered the markets anyway and began to make inroads into Gillette's position. Gillette needed to diversify – and to step up the rate of innovation.

The company's fastest growing market is oral hygiene. The Oral-B toothbrush system is a flagship brand, in both the manual and electric toothbrush categories. Gillette see their most lucrative strategy as being to encourage consumers to trade up – in world terms, most men who shave use double-edged blades. In these markets, Gillette seek to move these consumers onto better-performing twin blades or to twin-blade disposables. In mature markets, where the bulk of men are already using twin blade or disposables, the company offers triple blade systems. Customers of Oral-B manual toothbrushes can be traded up to the electric systems, customers for zinc carbon batteries can be encouraged to switch to Duracell, and Duracell customers can be moved up to the more advanced Duracell batteries.

Overall, Gillette has a well-planned, long-standing strategic plan for NPD and diffusion. Innovation is not a haphazard process: every product has its place in the plan.

Questions

1. How did Gillette develop his original idea for a disposable razor blade?
2. Why does the company innovate so much?
3. How does Gillette handle the problem of new products cannibalising sales of existing products?
4. What was the relationship between marketing and production in the case of the original blades?
5. How might trading up work in global markets?

ACTIVITY

Find out how NPD happens in your own firm, or a firm with which you are familiar. How does it relate to the standard model shown above? If it is different, do the differences make it work better or worse? What might be the reasons for senior management adopting a different approach from the standard one?

If you work for a small firm, the NPD process might well happen mainly inside someone's head – usually the boss. What are the problems with this approach?

ADOPTION OF INNOVATION

The adoption of innovation, whether of services or of physical products, is not an instantaneous process throughout the target market. Sales of products grow over a period of time, as evidenced by the product life cycle model. The delay in adoption is caused by a number of factors: word needs to get round that the product exists at all, some people are reluctant to try a new product until they have seen it in action (perhaps seen a friend using one), some people like to wait until any problems with the product have been identified and fixed, and some people are put off by the cost of switching from one product to another.

Switching cost is a key factor in adoption because it adds directly to the price. Someone considering a new product will almost certainly already have another solution that works adequately and will have to go to the trouble of learning how to use the new product, perhaps adapting his or her existing life, and perhaps have to spend money on accessories to make the new product work effectively. For example, someone buying a new mobile phone will probably already have a phone which works adequately and which might represent a considerable investment. The new phone will have new features which have to be learned, owner's current address book will have to be transferred across, and it may be necessary to buy a new carrying case or even new software to make the best use of the phone. The company selling the new phone will have to accept that the total price the customer pays (from the customer's viewpoint) will include these extra costs. This will inevitably affect the firm's pricing policy (another example of the way in which the 7Ps impinge on each other – in this case, how product policy affects price).

As products spread through the market, it is possible to distinguish between the different groups of consumers who buy at each stage. These are generally thought to be as follows:

- **Innovators.** These people like to be the first to own a new product, and they will probably pay a premium price in order to do so. They account for around 2.5% of the target market.

- **Early adopters.** These people are eager to adopt new products and will do so once the product has been on the market for a while. They account for about 13.5% of the market.

- **Early majority.** These people like to wait until the product has been available for some time, so that teething problems have been resolved, and they have had a chance to see the product in action. They account for around 33% of the market, so that we are now at the point where half the people in the potential target market have adopted the product.

- **Late majority.** These people only buy when the majority of people already have the product. They are wary of the new product and only feel confident to buy it when it is well established. They account for a further 33% of the market.

- **Laggards.** These people are reluctant to buy anything new and will only adopt the product if they are forced to. In some cases, they do not adopt at all: they account for the remainder of the market.

The adoption sequence does not tell us much about the individuals concerned, since there is no evidence that an adopter for one category of product would be an adopter for a different category. People who do not buy the latest computer games may simply not be interested in computer games under any circumstances: perhaps the same individual spends his or her spare time listening to music and would be an eager buyer of the latest hi-fi equipment. As a predictor, the model is therefore not very helpful: it does provide us with terminology, however, and it can be useful in terms of planning the style and content of marketing communications, since we can observe the product moving through the adoption process and can tailor our appeal appropriately.

EXAM TIP

You will be expected to know the correct terms for these adopter groups and know the order in which they adopt. If you can also remember the approximate proportions each group represents of the total market, it will gain you marks. You are likely to be asked to make recommendations about new product launches, and knowing the terminology will undoubtedly be expected of you.

Do not forget, though, that the divisions between the groups are arbitrary – they were decided on by a statistical process, not by looking at the personal characteristics of the individuals involved. Research into what makes someone want to adopt a new product is somewhat inconclusive – innovators can only really be defined by the fact that they buy new products, which is of course a fine example of circular reasoning.

MARKETING IN PRACTICE:
James Dyson

When James Dyson was a 23-year-old student at the Royal College of Art in London, he designed a novel boat, the Seatruck, which was able to carry cargo at high speeds. This won a Design Council award and went on to earn $500 million in sales. Dyson later invented the ballbarrow, a wheelbarrow with a ball instead of a wheel (which made it less likely to sink in soft earth), a boat launcher using balls instead of wheels, and an amphibious vehicle for use on sand dunes and on the sea.

Eventually, though, Dyson invented the product which made him a household name – the Dyson vacuum cleaner. This cleaner was the first bagless cleaner: needing no bag, it is cheaper to own and use and never loses suction. Dyson has promoted these benefits very ably, using advertisements showing people in the familiar position of having to dismantle the vacuum cleaner to find out what is clogging it up.

Dyson's success has been based on his ability to see the drawbacks with existing products and engineer solutions. His most successful inventions (the ballbarrow, the seatruck and the vacuum cleaner) have been based on their practical advantages over existing products. The Wheelboat amphibian has been less successful – and Dyson has had many other inventions which failed to make a hit with the public. Perhaps this is because they are technically interesting, but lack a practical advantage over existing products.

Whatever the reason, Dyson continues to invent. He recently launched a washing machine which does not tangle clothes and is working on improvements to his vacuum cleaners. The inventions are not revolutionary, but they are practical and do improve the lives of millions of people – simply because they meet people's needs better than the competing products.

Products will only be accepted if they offer benefits which existing products do not have. Many new ideas have been launched, only to disappear without trace because they do not have an advantage over products which are already on the market. New products are not necessarily either new or not new: there are degrees of newness, and one of the commonest classifications is that proposed by Robertson (1967), as follows (Figure 3.5):

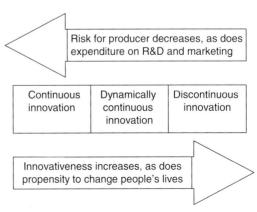

FIGURE 3.5 *Degrees of innovation.*

1. **Continuous innovation.** This is a new product which follows on from a previous version and is recognisably derived from its predecessor. Heavy-duty batteries, toothpaste with a built-in mouthwash, low-calorie biscuits and squeezable ketchup bottles are examples.

2. **Dynamically continuous innovation.** These products are new ways of solving old problems, but they do not make radical changes to the way people live. For example, DVD recorders do not change people's lives in the way that home video recorders did: they simply replaced the old technology with something which works better.

3. **Discontinuous innovation.** These are genuine new-to-the-world products that make radical changes to people's lives. Home computers and the Internet have changed the ways in which people communicate, study and work: mobile telephones have changed how people work and live. For earlier generations, the car, television, radio and aeroplane revolutionised ordinary people's lives.

Risk for the firm increases as newness increases, but so too do the potential returns. Continuous innovation rarely leads to product failures, and it is relatively easy to research consumer acceptance of a new model of an existing product: discontinuous innovations often fail (some researchers estimate that eight out of ten do not recover their development costs) and are virtually impossible to research since most people are unlikely to recognise the advantages until they have seen other people using the product.

Discontinuous innovations are risky, but on the plus side they do offer what is called the first-to-market advantage. A company which can produce something entirely new to the world will have a long lead time to gain market share while competitors try to develop competing products: sometimes patent protection will enable such firms to capture most of a market before the patent expires or competitors find a way around it.

There are six broad types of innovation strategy, as follows:

1. **Offensive.** Some firms aim to be the leading innovators in their industry (Sony is an example). Such firms seek to gain first-to-market advantage by spending a great deal of money and effort on developing new products.

2. **Defensive.** Companies following a defensive strategy will usually wait until a more innovative firm has introduced a radical new product, then produce their own version of it, incorporating some improvements. This often works well because any new product on the market is almost certainly going to have some faults which the

defensive company can exploit. The purpose of the exercise is to defend their own markets against the other company.

3. **Imitative.** This strategy involves making almost exact copies of new products. The strategy only works of the new product has weak, or no, patent protection: this is not the same as counterfeiting, which means passing off a copy as if it were made by the brand-owning company. Counterfeiting is illegal in most countries, whereas imitation is not unless there is good patent or copyright protection.

4. **Dependent.** Some companies only innovate as a result of being told to do so by a major customer. For example, a light engineering company might be contracted to produce components for a major car manufacturer and might be given an exact specification for a new component.

5. **Traditional.** This strategy is not really innovative at all, since it involves re-creating old traditional designs. For example, Victorian baked potato ovens staged a comeback a few years ago: the design was traditional, but it was a new product for the companies making the ovens.

6. **Opportunist.** Opportunist companies make and market new inventions as they become available, rather than having their own research and development systems. Inventors approach such companies with their ideas, taking a royalty on production as their payment.

CASE STUDY:
Innovations Catalogue

Innovations has almost become a UK institution. Launched in 1985, the catalogue offered gadgets and inventions of all descriptions to an unsuspecting public – the pioneer of the radio-controlled clock, the recharger for ordinary carbon–zinc batteries, the treeless hammock and the extendable window-cleaning device. The company also offered some less immediately useful devices: the fun-fur-lined golf club cover, the portable paper shredder and the one-size-fits-all galoshes.

In 2003, the catalogue appeared to be heading into the decline stage of the product life cycle. Its owners, Great Universal Stores, said that the catalogue was underperforming and had to be closed down. The Spring 2003 catalogue was the last – but the brand continued, shifting itself (inevitably) to the most modern of media, the Internet. Now part of Shop Direct Group, the Innovations mail-order service continues unchecked, offering lip-shaped pillows, patented oyster-openers and Toastabags (which allow people to make toasted sandwiches in an ordinary toaster).

Gadget lovers are attracted by the catalogue – a glance at the section which says 'customers who bought this also bought ...' reveals that customers for a novel folding bed also bought Toastabags and festive rubber gloves (washing-up gloves with Christmas tinsel on them). Not to mention Wormie, the colour-coded terracotta worm that tells you when to water your plants.

In fact, a trawl through the Innovations website is a real adventure for anyone who loves gadgets. Some are eminently sensible, some are incomprehensible, and some are clearly useful but somehow unappealing; most are novel and relatively few are traditional or resurrected designs. Innovations claim to have only one goal: to seek out the world's latest innovations and market them first. Innovations is an admirer of the lone inventor, toiling away in the garden shed, and is happy to advise inventors about how to bring their products to market.

The appeal of the catalogue to consumers has never really been clear. Because of its eclectic approach, Innovations offered products for everyone from gardeners to hi-fi enthusiasts: alongside products intended to make housework easier were products for the office, and on the next page to the electric coin-sorting machine were the advertisements for dog-hair removing equipment. Even the seafood-eating kit (obviously aimed at the gourmet market) appeared alongside the Air-Flow Mouse, a computer mouse with a built-in fan to keep the hands cool while surfing.

This lack of a clear target market may have been what killed the paper catalogue, but it does not appear to be a problem for the online version. Products are arranged by category – gadgets, health and fitness, car and travel, home and garden, sound and vision, and what's new. This still begs the question of how the catalogue is targeted.

Throughout its life, Innovations has provided a talking point for people. Because of the novelty of its products, people have actually read the catalogue and often told friends about products – often in a sense of poking fun at some of the more outlandish gadgets, but nonetheless talking. Almost everybody in the United Kingdom has heard of the Innovations catalogue and knows what it has to offer (at least in a broad sense), and most people have browsed through at one time or another. Obviously, enough people stop and buy items for the catalogue to have remained viable for 20 years – and equally obviously there is no shortage of ideas for new products to fill its pages.

Case study questions

1. How might Innovations seek to overcome the problem of not having a clear target market?
2. What might be the appeal of Innovations to the average person?
3. What factors have enabled Innovations to maintain its success?
4. Why would somebody buy fun-fur-lined golf club covers?

ACTIVITY

Find three or more products from the Innovations catalogue, or from a gadget shop, or on the Strange New Products website (the URL is given at the end of this unit).

What need does each product address? What might people be doing already to meet that need? Why is the new product better at meeting the need? What might be the costs of adopting the new product (purchase price and switching costs)? Do you think the product would be viable in the long term, and if not, why not?

PRICE

Price is often regarded as one of the least interesting aspects of marketing, but in fact it is crucially important to the firm to set the right price for a product. This is for the following reasons:

1. Price brings together the other elements of the marketing mix and affects each one of them. For example, price is often used by consumers to judge the likely quality of the product (a product function), and price can also be used as a short-term incentive to buy (a promotion function). Price can also be used to encourage people to buy online (a process function).

2. Price determines the firm's income and profits for each product and each market. A relatively small increase in price can lead to a very large increase in profits, unless of course the higher price means customers buy competing products instead.

3. Price contributes to the firm's business and financial objectives. Pitching a low price will probably increase unit sales (at the cost of losing profit), so price can be used to control demand, perhaps in order to maintain efficient use of production capacity. This is particularly important in service industries, where the product cannot be stockpiled – this is why many restaurants offer early-evening discounts or weekday discounts to use capacity at less popular times. Controlling demand in this way is sometimes called loading: the same result can be achieved by increasing customer value, perhaps by offering a free aperitif to early diners.

4. Price can operate as a competitive tool – with care. Competing by reducing prices can lead to retaliation by competitors, and a price war will always favour the firm with the most cash resources.

Because price has an immediate effect on the value proposition, it can be used to boost sales temporarily (e.g. a sales promotion which offers a discount). The drawback with this is that cutting the price has a dramatic effect on profits – if, for example, the company has a 20% profit margin, a cut of 10% off the price to the customer (which is a relatively small discount in some markets) results in halving the supplier's profit margin. In most cases, competing on price is just a quick way to lose money. On the other hand, raising the price by 10% (a figure which may go unnoticed by buyers in some markets) increases profits by 50%.

Price is an important surrogate for judging quality. People tend to assume that the higher priced product is better quality, and if the price/quality ratio is right, higher priced products actually represent better value for money since they offer more benefits: people often think that paying extra is worthwhile in order to obtain a better product. Of course, the product has to meet the customers' expectations, or no repeat purchases will result.

Relatively few people consistently buy the cheapest products. People only do this if the reasons for buying a more expensive product are not immediately apparent, in other words if advertising or point-of-sale materials have been inadequate to explain why one product is superior to another. If this were not so, the most popular cars on the road would be cheap Eastern European models or basic cars such as the Fiat Seicento. In fact, the most popular car in Europe in 2006 was the Opel Astra, selling almost half a million vehicles: the tenth most popular was the BMW 3 series, which is of course a premium-priced car. Since the BMW out-sold many cheaper, more basic vehicles such as the Ford Mondeo and the Renault Megane, it is obvious that a large number of people are prepared to pay more for a better product and consider the BMW to be better value for money than the Ford or the Renault.

CASE STUDY:
The International
Software Market

Computer software is an unusual product. It is entirely intangible, and the costs of supplying it can also be negligible – it is the cost of writing it in the first place which is the main expense. Once the software exists, the costs of putting it onto CDs and packaging it are tiny in comparison. Still cheaper is distribution over the Internet – which is why there is so much free software available online.

Software is also easily copied by pirates, which makes life difficult for major software companies, and also each company seeks to make its own software the industry standard, so that they can sell upgrades and add-ons. The switching costs for someone who has adopted a particular company's software can be high, so there is a considerable advantage in being the first software a customer commits to.

The situation is further complicated by international marketing. Obviously, the software company needs to make an overall profit and therefore generate a substantial turnover from worldwide sales of the software, but on the other hand customers in the wealthy countries of Western Europe, the United States and Australia can afford to pay much more than customers in the developing world such as India, parts of Asia and Africa. At the same time, computers are a global phenomenon, so it pays for companies to ensure that each country uses the same systems. In other words, it is worthwhile to subsidise poorer countries, because it helps adoptions in wealthier countries.

This creates a nightmarish problem for software marketers. Setting a price which people will pay is one thing, but ensuring that people in the wealthier countries do not feel that they are being cheated is another. For major players such as Sun Microsystems and Microsoft, the stakes are high – customers in the developing world are numbered in the billions, and in the software industry plans for world domination are constantly on the agenda. Companies that do not dominate will go to the wall – there is no room for second-best. Microsoft always operated on a one-price basis – everybody paid the same, whatever country they were in. This ensured that customers in the developed world did not feel cheated and also prevented software from being bought in one country for use in another. However, as the 21st century began, it became obvious that this position would not be tenable in the long run. Something would have to change in Microsoft's pricing!

Companies in the software business have been forced to use differential pricing (using a different price in each market for the same product) in developing countries, simply because a price tag of $90 seems very expensive in countries where most people only earn an average of $2 a day. Even though people who can afford a computer are in much higher income brackets, the temptation to buy pirated software is high.

Microsoft's answer to this was to introduce cut-down versions of Windows XP specifically adapted for the developing world. In December 2004, the company began offering versions of XP in the local language, with some features removed, in India, Russia, Malaysia and Indonesia. The product had already been piloted in Thailand and had been greeted with great enthusiasm. Microsoft's Kenneth Lundin said that the move was intended to give more people access to software and also reduce the incidence of pirating of software. Because the cut-down XP systems are only available in the local language, grey-market copies were unlikely to be shipped out to the wealthier Western markets, and also the software was only being made available to computer manufacturers – not to the general public. This means that the software either comes ready-installed on the computer or is protected so that it can only be installed once. Microsoft have agreed this as part of a deal with the Malaysian Government, intended to increase the use of computers in the country from its current 15% of the population to 35%. The company is understandably

coy about exactly how much it is charging for the software, but since the simplified computers sell for around £350, the software has to be a lot cheaper than the £100-plus price tag of the UK version.

At the same time, Sun Microsystems are entering the business sector with a version of its Java software. Sun are using a unique pricing system, based on the number of people in the country and the country's state of development as verified by the United Nations. John Loiacano, executive vice-president of software at Sun, said: 'With our new per citizen pricing model, governments of developing nations can now reallocate punitive software licensing fees to critical tasks such as healthcare and education. And the expanded platform support allows these nations to deliver network services to citizens and customers on the architecture of their choice.'

Both companies are suggesting that their actions are at least partly philanthropic: Microsoft talk about extending the benefits of computer ownership to the poorer nations, and Loiacano of Sun talks about allowing countries to spend their money on hospitals and schools rather than on education. Seeking the moral high ground is, of course, fine and what the company spokesmen say is quite true – but the fact remains that both companies have now won a captive market for their software, probably for the next 20 or 30 years at least. In Malaysia alone, Microsoft look set to pick up around 3 million new customers – and Malaysia has a population of only 26 million.

Questions

1. What is the role of consumer characteristics in software price setting?

2. Why should companies not charge one price for everyone, regardless of location?

3. Why might the product not represent the same value for money in each of its markets?

4. The market is huge, so why is there not room for many players to compete?

5. How might a new software supplier (e.g. an Indian or Chinese supplier) price its products effectively in the world market?

MARKETING IN PRACTICE:
Lucie's Farm

Farmers in the United Kingdom often have a hard time. They are price takers, not price makers, because the market decides the prices (on the basis of supply and demand), and no one farmer is large enough to affect demand or supply – and since farmers are dependent on the weather so much, the supply is largely determined by the British climate, which is uncertain at best (and certainly bad at worst).

Escaping from the tedious cycle of failed crops, uncertain European Union subsidies, and ever-rising costs and paperwork has proved difficult or even impossible for most farmers. Some, however, like Craig and Marjorie Walsh, have found a way to break out of the ever-decreasing circle.

In 1985, the couple saw the movie Rob Roy and were so impressed with the Highland cattle in the film they decided to breed them. They are now the leading Highland Cattle breeders outside Scotland and are happy to sell the animals for meat, or for breeding or (perhaps spectacularly) as 'lawn ornaments' for wealthy people with large gardens. What has helped Craig and Marjorie escape the price-taker trap is the fact that they produce beef to a very high standard. Their beef is aged for 21 days after slaughter – about 3–4 times as long as the average pre-packed supermarket steak – and is organically reared. The flavour and tenderness of their beef is already legendary, but the couple recently went a stage further and began producing Kobe-style beef.

Kobe beef originates in Japan and is produced from cattle which are treated better than royalty. The cattle drink beer from the local microbrewery, eat grain and are regularly massaged with sake to make the beef tender. The end result is an incredibly tender, delicious meat – which of course sells for a premium price! Craig and Marjorie's farm, Lucie's Farm in Worcestershire, is a Mecca for restaurateurs and foodies prepared to pay around £60 for enough meat for four people (even four hamburger patties comes out to around £12).

In an affluent society, there will always be a market for the 'special treat', and even for luxurious foods on a daily basis. Lucie's Farm, by adding value to the product, has tapped into that market extremely successfully.

Taking control of pricing, as in the case of Lucie's Farm, is an important factor in competition. Competing on price (i.e. trying to be the cheapest in the market) is unlikely to be as effective as competing on value for money, since it is very simple for competitors to retaliate by cutting their own prices. In practice there will always be a competitor who is able to cut prices to the bone – even to the point where they are losing money – if they are desperate to retain market share.

Adding to the customer value (what the customer gets in exchange for the price paid) is a much safer alternative, provided the value added is greater for the consumer than the price increase entailed, and the cost of adding the value is less than the premium charged. If this is the case, both sales and profits will increase.

STUDY TIP

It is worth bearing in mind that the price people are prepared to pay for a product bears no relationship whatsoever to the cost of making the product. Ultimately it is the price people are prepared to pay which will determine what can be charged.

You can probably think of many examples of this – the price of T-shirts which cost pennies to make is sometimes as high as £10. Having some examples in mind is useful in exams, but it is even more useful to your career, as you will often find yourself in the position of defending customer-based pricing in the face of engineers and accountants who are more likely to favour cost-based pricing.

PRICING METHODS

You will be expected to understand different methods of pricing and be able to apply them: you may well be asked to compare the advantages and disadvantages of each method, and to make recommendations as to which approach to pricing is most appropriate in any given set of circumstances. In the 'real world', you will need to understand pricing methods in order to argue your case with colleagues, many of whom will have been taught pricing approaches which are not customer orientated.

The following are the categories of method you will need to understand:

- **Absorption costing.** This method prices according to a formula which includes all the costs of producing the product, including an allowance for overheads. It takes no account at all of what customers are prepared to pay, so it is not a market-orientated approach.

- **Cost base and marginal costing.** These again start from the costs the firm incurs, but this time the price is set at the point where producing one more unit of production would not be profitable. In practice, this is extremely difficult to calculate and again takes no account whatsoever of customers.

- **Cost plus pricing.** This is the method most accountants and engineers are taught. It involves calculating the costs of production for a given production run, then adding on a fixed percentage for the profit. It is not market orientated, since it takes no account of competitors or of what customers might be prepared to pay.

- **Demand pricing.** This method is customer orientated, because prices are set at a level which will ensure that demand for the product is at a point which will meet corporate objectives. For example, a company may be able to produce economically at a particular level, so the price will be set to ensure that demand reaches that level, no more and no less. Alternatively, demand pricing can be used to determine the point at which profit will be maximised, that is, the point at which a further increase in price will reduce the production run past the most economical point, or a reduction in price will simply reduce profit without materially affecting sales.

- **Penetration pricing.** Here the company sets prices low in order to capture a large part of the market before competitors can respond. This is a dangerous policy unless the company has very large resources: the risk of starting a damaging price war is high, and of course profits will be minimal or even negative, that is, a loss will be incurred. In some contexts, penetration pricing is illegal, because it represents unfair competition; in international markets, it is known as dumping or predatory pricing.

- **Skimming.** The company sets the price high initially so as to 'skim' the consumers who are prepared to pay a premium to be the first to own a new product. The price is then gradually reduced so as to 'skim' consumers who are prepared to pay a lesser price and so forth. This method is commonly used in consumer electronics markets, where the company has a technical lead which can be maintained long enough to shut out competitors. Unfortunately, most consumers know enough about marketing to realise that the price will fall if they are prepared to wait, so they often delay purchase.

- **Loss leader.** Some retailers will offer some basic commodities at a price which will actually lose money in order to lure customers into the store. Inevitably people will buy other goods while in the store as well as the loss leader, and the store makes its money on these other purchases. This principle has been carried over into other marketing situations – for example, companies manufacturing printers for home computers sell the printers for less than the price of replacement ink cartridges and make their profit on the ink.

- **Promotional pricing.** In order to even out demand or bring sales forward for other reasons, firms often offer extra discounts or 'sale prices'. Because such promotions cut profits, it may be cheaper to offer some other kind of promotion, but promotional pricing does have the advantage of being quick to put in place, and it is also very effective very quickly.

- **Odd–even pricing.** This is the practice of ending the price with 99p or 95c. Some studies have shown that this adds 8% to sales volumes, while other studies are less conclusive: certainly, it is less effective in some markets. An extension of this type of pricing is found in China, where some numbers are regarded as lucky: collectively, pricing which creates perceptions of this type is called psychological pricing.

EXAM HINT

You are likely to be asked about the pricing of new products. If so, you should bear in mind that penetration pricing is extremely risky: it will almost always trigger a competitive response, and therefore a price war. Price wars are extremely damaging to profit margins, and sometimes companies end up bankrupt as the firm with the greatest level of reserves can undercut for the longest period of time. In some circumstances, penetration pricing may be illegal, if it is seen as unfair competition.

Many students imagine that cutting prices is the best way to compete. In most cases, it is probably the worst way to compete: it is certainly avoided by the vast majority of companies, because it cuts profits and it signals poor quality to the consumers. Incidentally, there is a general point here: whatever recommendations you make, you will need to consider competitive response. Competitors will not stand by and let you eat their lunch!

CASE STUDY:
Internet Auctions

The Internet has opened up many opportunities for increasing consumer power, and nowhere has this been more apparent than in the proliferation of Internet auction sites. Sellers are able to post goods for sale on sites such as eBay or eBid, with or without a reserve price, and buyers are able to place their bids from (theoretically) anywhere in the world. The price rises as more people bid, until there is only one buyer left, who then buys the product at the final bid price. Buyers can pay by credit card through an escrow company (which holds the funds until the goods are delivered) or can make arrangements directly with the seller for payment.

In recent years, the process has moved a step further with the advent of reverse auctions. Firms such as Letsbuyit.com bring buyers together to bid for products. The philosophy is simple: rather than bidding against other purchasers, and forcing the price up, the reverse auction arranges for buyers to join together and force the price down. For example, a manufacturer may offer an LCD TV for £800. If, however, 100 people are prepared to place a single order, the price might drop to £600. If 200 people are prepared to buy, the price might drop to £500. The price paid to the supplier will be dictated by the number of buyers, so Letsbuyit.com begins by negotiating a series of steps at which the price will fall. The prices are posted on the website for a set period, but once the product is sold out it will not be available to later bidders. If the number of people wishing to buy the product does not meet a pre-set

minimum, the purchase does not go ahead, and the bidders pay nothing. Those who bid therefore run the risk of getting nothing: on the other hand, if the deal goes through, they will undoubtedly walk away with a real bargain.

The implications of this for traditional High Street retailers are potentially extremely damaging. Although they might argue that consumers will still prefer to come to a store where they are able to examine the products, get advice from the staff and even try out products, there is obviously nothing to stop consumers doing this and then making the actual purchase via a reverse auction. The implications for manufacturers are equally far reaching: although the power of retailers will be curtailed, which for many manufacturers would be a godsend, the power of consumers is likely to increase dramatically.

On the one hand, reverse auctions offer manufacturers a kind of instant marketing research; on the other hand, the process may mean the end of price skimming, psychological pricing and all the other tried-and-tested techniques for maximising the profitability of innovative products.

In some cases, consumers have gone even further by cutting out the Internet service provider altogether. They have taken to send tenders to car dealers and other retailers asking them to bid for supplying the product. On a new-car purchase, an astute logged-on consumer might save hundreds or even thousands of pounds in this way –

a saving that more than compensates for a few minutes spent sending out e-mails.

If these consumer-led techniques catch on, the outcomes are by no means entirely bad for manufacturers, but the overall effect is a major change in the way pricing is carried out. Prices are much more directly controlled by the end consumer than ever before – and marketers need to adjust to that fact.

Case study questions

1. How might a manufacturer retain a skimming policy when dealing with a reverse auction?

2. How might a car dealer encourage a prospective customer to increase the tender price?

3. What advantages might there be for manufacturers in participating in reverse auctions?

4. How might a manufacturer calculate the appropriate price bands for a reverse auction?

5. What might retailers do to counteract the effects of reverse auctions?

DISTRIBUTION CHANNELS

Getting the product into the right place, at the right time and in the right condition for customers to buy it is the 'place' element of the marketing mix. Many firms have differentiated themselves entirely on the place element: Avon Cosmetics, for example, broke new ground by selling products door-to-door rather than through department stores and pharmacies. By so doing, the company opened up an entirely new market among women who were housebound for whatever reason.

There are various players in the distribution process, as follows:

- **Wholesalers.** These firms carry out a number of useful functions in terms of bulk breaking of large shipments, assorting different types of product into convenient quantities for shipping out, and so forth: they buy goods themselves and sell them on, but not to the final consumers.

- **Retailers.** These intermediaries sell to final consumers. They may or may not operate from a store: mail order and Internet retailing are also retailers. Any organisation which sells to end users is a retailer, whatever the medium involved.

- **Agents.** These people do not buy goods themselves, but they do act as go-betweens, selling manufacturers' goods to wholesalers and retailers. Agents can be particularly useful in overseas markets, where they know the local laws and customs and have local knowledge: often an agent can save a small firm from having to set up warehousing and marketing operations overseas.

- **Export houses and import houses.** These firms specialise in buying or selling goods from other countries. They may or may not take possession of the goods – in many cases, goods are shipped directly from the producer to the foreign wholesaler.

There are several other types of intermediary, but the following routes allow the supplier to remove intermediaries from the equation altogether and sell directly to consumers.

- **Direct marketing.** This is a set of techniques by which products are promoted via a medium which allows a direct response from the customer, for example, a press advertisement which contains a coupon, or a mailing which contains a reply-paid order form.

- **Vending machines.** These allow people to purchase directly from the machine, using coins or (in some cases) credit cards. Vending machines need to be filled with product and emptied of cash, of course, and also the site owners will charge a rental, so the overall cost might be higher than using a traditional retail route. What vending machines do best is provide access to places traditional retailers might have trouble reaching – station platforms, office corridors, factory floors and so forth.

- **Telephone selling.** Generally considered to be a part of direct marketing, telephone selling can be inbound (customers call as a result of seeing a marketing communication) or outbound (customers are called by telesales operators). Outbound telesales has proved extremely unpopular with consumers in recent years, and verbal attacks on telesales operators mean that staff turnover is high and stress levels can become excessive. Some firms have relocated their call centres overseas, which has two advantages: first, costs are likely to be lower if the call centre is relocated to a low-wage economy, and second, time-zone differences sometimes mean that a 24-hour service can be maintained without requiring staff to work through the night. Again, overseas call centres have proved unpopular with the public, partly because of concerns about security and partly because of concerns about job losses in the United Kingdom.

- **Franchising.** A business franchisor offers exclusive rights to a franchisee to use the corporate brand name within a specific geographical area or other segment. McDonald's is probably the best-known example of a franchise: such businesses are closely regulated by the franchisor to ensure that the brand values remain intact.

- **Electronic retailing.** Online retailing is becoming more and more commonplace as consumers become more Internet-literate. There are drawbacks: delivery of goods can be problematic, especially to people who are not at home, and mistakes happen when people are using unfamiliar websites.

Because intermediaries usually add value by the various activities they undertake, it is often not beneficial to cut them out of the picture. For example, a cash-and-carry wholesaler adds place value for small retailers or caterers. They are able to obtain most or all of their supplies in one place, which is a considerable saving in time and effort: cutting out the wholesaler would mean that each producer would have to deliver to each retailer, probably in uneconomic quantities, and giving the retailer the problem of dealing with a constant stream of deliveries happening at all times of the day.

The value added by each intermediary will be greater than the profit margin 'charged', otherwise other intermediaries will quickly appear to replace the inefficient one.

STUDY TIP

It is very common for people to talk about 'cutting out the middle man' as a way of reducing the cost of goods. After all, wholesalers and other intermediaries do add on a profit for themselves. However, the efficiency gained by having a single point for shipments, plus help with marketing goods (sometimes into specialist markets) more than compensates for the profit added. Therefore, removing intermediaries (disintermediation) almost always increases costs.

Familiarise yourself with various channels of distribution and consider which would be most suitable for each of several categories of product.

CASE STUDY:
C. A. Papaellina & Co. Ltd.

Cyprus is an island in the Eastern Mediterranean, perhaps best known as a holiday destination: the party-and-package holiday resort of Ayia Napa, the Troodhos Mountains, the family resort of Paphos in the west and the ancient Greek and Egyptian ruins on the island are world-famous. Cyprus has a considerable military presence also: since 1974, the island has been divided between the Turkish Cypriots in the North and the Greek Cypriots in the South, with the United Nations maintaining an uneasy truce between the two along the Green Line, which divides Nicosia into two. The island's strategic situation, close to the Middle East, means that the British Army and the RAF maintain large bases on the island at Akrotiri and Dhekalia. Although there has been some relaxation of the Green Line in recent years (with a permanent crossing-point opened up on 5 April 2008), the island still remains divided.

Cyprus has a small population (around 760,000 people) but is economically highly successful, with a high standard of living and low unemployment (around 3.4%). It thus represents a desirable, though small, market for most consumer goods. Greek Cyprus is now part of the European Union, and if reunification talks go as well as is hoped, the Northern part of the island will also benefit from EU membership. The island is small: the Greek part of the island is less than 70 miles from end to end, and around 30 miles wide at the widest point.

C.A. Papaellina & Co. Ltd. (or CAP) is one of the island's most important distributors. CAP was founded in 1930 and has since grown to the point where the company distributes into most of the retail outlets on the island. The company is well aware of the peculiarities of the Cypriot distribution system: for example, the island has many small street-corner kiosks which sell everything from newspapers to bootlaces, as well as several huge hypermarkets (retail stores of over 5,000 square metres selling area). CAP handles many international brands, such as Chanel, Davidoff, Jean Paul Gaultier, Kleenex, Lucozade, Ribena, Aquafresh, Maclean's and even Tabasco Sauce. In 2002, the company opened its new pharmaceuticals centre, and in 2001, it signed a contract for new warehouse software worth CYP170,000 (approximately $300,000). This software was supplied by the UK software house, JBA Automated Systems of Durham.

CAP is divisionalised into five separate areas, as follows:

1. Personal care and household products

2. Consumer health care products

3. Paper products and foodstuffs

4. Cosmetics and Fragrances

5. Pharmaceuticals

CAP employs 150 people, runs its own sales force and supplies in every retail sector in Cyprus. This means that the firm is equally able to supply huge hypermarkets and corner kiosks – in itself, this presents considerable logistical and accounting problems. Using its own fleet of trucks and vans, the company distributes throughout the Greek portion of the island.

Because the Cypriot market is so small, distribution chains are short and often integrated (i.e. members own shares in each others' companies): CAP owns 30% of the AlphaMega Hypermarket in Nicosia, 100% of Beautyline (the cosmetics retail chain) and 50% of Demetrides and Papaellinas, the distributors for the Swiss pharmaceutical giant, Novartis. CAP opened its own specialist pharmaceutical distribution centre, PharmacyLine, in March 2002. This distribution centre can carry out daily deliveries to every pharmacy in Cyprus, an important service considering that many medicines have extremely short shelf lives or may be in infrequent demand and therefore may not be stocked by the pharmacies.

Foreign companies appreciate the way CAP uses its intimate knowledge of the Cypriot market to facilitate distribution. For example, CAP has a re-labelling and re-packing unit in which imported products are re-labelled in Greek to meet local labelling requirements and if necessary are also repackaged. CAP's knowledge of the local distribution systems means that the company is able to distribute in bulk to hypermarkets with the same ease with which its small vans distribute small quantities to kiosks: the mountainous topography of Cyprus and its constant influx of foreign visitors present special problems which only a local firm can solve.

Cyprus is a small island dependent on foreign trade. It can no longer be self-sufficient, but it is rich, so it imports most of what it needs from day to day and exports some agricultural products and a lot of tourism. C.A. Papaellina is at the forefront of facilitating this exchange.

Case study questions

1. What advantages does Novartis gain from dealing through CAP?

2. Why might CAP have bought into retail outlets?

3. What specific problems might a confectionery manufacturer have when approaching the Cypriot market? How might CAP be able to help?

4. What are the major differences between supplying hypermarkets and supplying kiosks?

5. Why would competing manufacturers such as Chanel and Jean Paul Gaultier be prepared to use the same distributor?

EXAM TIP

If you are asked about distribution channels, you will be expected to understand the strengths and weaknesses of different approaches. Short distribution channels give more control to the producer, but are often less efficient and increase costs. Ensure that, if asked a question which involves distribution, you consider both the strategic aspects of channel choice and the role of logistics in getting products to customers.

Distribution falls into two main areas: choosing the right channels and physical distribution (or logistics) which is concerned with transporting products to the right locations. Choosing the right channels through which to send goods is a strategic decision based on the choice of target market and the product characteristics, whereas logistics is a set of tactical decisions which involve transport decisions, warehouse decisions and financial decisions. Logistics is also based on product characteristics, as well as market infrastructures and market conditions.

The next case study considers logistics. Logistical issues include the following decision areas:

- **The possibility of using multiple channels**, which means a different delivery system for each channel. For example, a food manufacturer might have one system for delivering to caterers (perhaps through a cash and carry warehouse), another for delivering to supermarkets (perhaps direct delivery using the company's own trucks), and still another for independent grocers. Multiple channels need to be handled carefully, since some channel members (e.g. wholesalers) might feel that they are being bypassed and therefore undermined.

- **Location of customers.** Customers in remote locations will need different physical distribution solutions from those located in urban areas. Obviously, a global market will require special measures.

- **Compatibility.** The selected delivery method must be compatible with the channel, the product, the customers and the supplier. Some customers will need rapid, reliable deliveries (spare parts delivery to car repairers being one example), whereas for other customers rapid delivery is less important than, say, reliable delivery times.

- **Nature of the goods/services.** Perishable goods clearly need to be delivered more quickly (and probably therefore more expensively) than non-perishables. Often air freight is actually cheaper than surface transport for items such as fresh fruit or fish because there is less wastage.

- **Geography, environment and terrain.** Clearly deliveries into northern Alaska require different techniques from deliveries into Iquitos in Peru: apart from the obvious climatic differences, Iquitos has no road access to the outside world, so everything has to be delivered either by river or by air.

- **Storage and distribution costs.** Warehousing can be an expensive issue, hence the idea of just-in-time purchasing by which components are delivered in small batches, theoretically at the exact time they are needed in the factory, thus avoiding the cost of managing a store. Just-in-time has fallen into disrepute in recent years because it often results in trucks waiting outside the factory gates for the exact moment to deliver, resulting in greater waste on the part of the supplying company.

- ■ **Import/export costs.** Apart from transport costs, there may be customs duties to pay on goods, and there will always be international insurance payments to make.

CASE STUDY: Giant Bicycles

In 1972, the Giant Manufacturing Company was first established in Taiwan, producing bicycles for the local market. In fact, the company was not giant at all at that time, but the name proved to be a prophetic one because within 8 years Giant was the largest bicycle company in Taiwan and was looking to expand internationally.

An obvious overseas market for Giant was the Netherlands, where everybody owns at least one bicycle and the entire country is networked by bicycle tracks. In 1986, Giant opened their first overseas sales office in Holland: in the following year, the company opened up in the United Kingdom and the United States, and by 1991 had offices in six overseas countries including Japan and Australia. Their first overseas factory was opened in the Netherlands in 1996.

Giant have had notable successes on the racing circuit and have their own race team: the team won the team prize in the Tour de France and the World Cup, and the company expects to build on this success in the future. The rapid expansion of the company has not been without its problems, however: despite a huge investment in IT, and a commitment to 'the local touch', the company still faced an enormous problem in terms of logistics.

Apart from having to consider local needs and tastes (e.g. Dutch cyclists predominantly use their bikes to commute to and from work, whereas Americans use their bikes for leisure and exercise), the company has been faced with the problem of shipping bikes worldwide from only three factories (Taiwan, China and the Netherlands). Because of the wide range of characteristics of cyclists (Dutch people are the tallest in the world: Japanese people are among the shortest), the company not only needs to produce a wide range of bikes, but also needs to ensure that stocks of bikes in the various retailers throughout the world can meet the demand. Giant makes over 3 million bicycles a year, but may need to deliver only one or two to a specific small retailer, perhaps in a remote area.

For Giant, the problem is complex. Worldwide distribution is difficult to arrange at the best of times, but given the huge variation in needs of customers, and the wide range of retail outlets which must be supplied, the company had a major logistics problem. Giant bikes are available on every continent, through over 10,000 retail outlets.

Giant therefore contacted Wincanton Group, a major European logistics company. Wincanton offer a full logistics service, including warehousing, intermodal transport (transport which involves different types of vehicle), customs clearance, document and records management, store services and even aircraft refuelling. Wincanton operate a fleet of vehicles, including lorries, barges and trains, and the company even manages sea ports and inland ports for barge transportation.

Wincanton's roots lie in the United Kingdom (it was originally a subsidiary of the dairy company that later became Cow and Gate), but its operations now cover almost the whole of Europe. The company handles logistics for major firms such as BMW, Tesco, Dow Chemicals, Electrolux and Hewlett–Packard, so shipping and storing bicycles presented no major problems.

Wincanton's success is due in no small measure to the company's innovative use of IT. Since Giant Bicycles also has a strong IT base, the companies were able to interface their systems and exchange data directly, greatly improving the efficiency of the overall system.

Giant Bicycles Ltd. is moving into the 21st century with more new products – an electrically assisted bicycle was introduced in 1999, followed by a range of models which are available worldwide. The company's innovative Maestro suspension system has proved to be hugely popular, and the company also makes folding bicycles. However, no matter how many new models the company produces, and no matter how many markets it targets, Wincanton is confident in being able to provide the necessary logistical support.

Questions

1. What are the advantages of using a firm like Wincanton?

2. How might Giant Bicycles enter markets where Wincanton are not represented?

3. What are the main problems Giant faces in terms of logistics?

4. What challenges does Wincanton face in the 21st century?

5. What type of information might the companies exchange via their mutual IT systems?

PROMOTION

Non-marketers tend to think of promotion as being the whole of marketing, and it is certainly the most visible area that marketers manage. Promotion encompasses all forms of marketing communication, so many marketing academics and managers use the term 'marketing communications' to cover promotion in general.

Promotion has its own system of subdivision, the promotional mix. In its most basic form, it consists of the following four elements:

- **Advertising.** This is the paid insertion of a message in a medium. There is therefore no such thing as free advertising: promotion which is 'free' might be classified as public relations or word of mouth, but it is not advertising. Although advertising is often thought of as the main element in marketing communication, it is actually only the most visible element: the other elements can be equally, or more, important and may even absorb more of the firm's resources. Advertising has the advantage that the marketers can control the content and to some extent the audience by choosing the most appropriate medium. The biggest drawback of advertising is that people find it relatively easy to avoid – they skip past the pages the advertising is on or change channels while the TV commercials are on. Advertising also suffers from a lack of credibility: people are aware that the advertiser has an agenda to follow and usually assume that the advertiser's needs will come ahead of the consumer's needs.

- **Public relations.** This is all the activities that create a positive image of the company and its brands – press releases, sponsorship, event management and so forth. Public relations is about creating an impression of a company that is good to do business with, but it does not directly bring in sales. Companies with a good PR record have little trouble in selling their goods, however – for example, imagine the difference between an IBM salesperson arriving at a new prospect's offices and a salesperson from some unknown computer company arriving at the same time. The IBM salesperson would almost certainly have a much more positive reception and would be taken seriously immediately, whereas the unknown salesperson would have to begin by establishing some credibility before even being allowed to discuss products. Public relations has a major advantage over advertising in that it is much more credible – a press release is read as news, sponsorship builds on the reputation of the sponsored person or event, and so forth.

- **Personal selling.** Probably the most powerful marketing tool, a salesperson calling on prospective customers to present the firm's products is also probably the most expensive tool, at least in terms of number of contacts made, but it has the major advantage that a salesperson can identify specific needs of a customer and propose suitable solutions from among the company's range of products. Top-class salespeople will often propose solutions from elsewhere as well, if the company's product range is insufficient. The important point to note about personal selling is that it is not about persuading people to buy things – it is about identifying and solving customer problems.

- **Sales promotion.** This includes money-off discounts, buy-one-get-one-free offers, extra fill of the pack and in fact anything intended to give a short-term boost to sales. In most cases, the switch from one brand to another caused by a sales promotion is only temporary: typically, people either switch back to their usual brand, or (in the case of bargain-hunters) switch to whichever brand is on offer this week. Sales promotions rarely increase sales overall – they are good for bringing sales forward (because people stock up) and are good for shutting out competition (sometimes this is a good thing to do at traditionally busy times, such as Christmas, because it damages competitors' sales at a time when they were expecting a high revenue stream).

In fact, the above list is far from comprehensive: in recent years, direct marketing has been added to the list by many commentators, but there are still many more promotion tools in the locker. Some of these are as follows:

- **Ambient advertising.** This is advertising which becomes part of the physical environment – messages on stair risers and petrol pump nozzles, art installations in city centres and so forth. Ambient advertising often cuts through advertising clutter (the effect of having so much advertising targeted at people that they simply ignore all of it). It also often has novelty value, so that people remember it and sometimes even tell their friends about it.

■ **Websites.** An Internet website can be interactive (almost all UK and American sites are interactive, but there are still some which are static, mainly in Eastern and Southern Europe). Websites offer an entirely different communications medium from any other, because they establish an automated dialogue with the customer. They therefore give the consumer a degree of control over the dialogue, whereas in most cases promotions are either one-way monologues in which the consumer has only a passive role, or managed by salespeople rather than by the customers.

■ **Word of mouth.** This is probably the most powerful promotional medium available, since it is the most likely to be believed and acted upon. Word of mouth is informal communication between friends and family members: people like to talk about products they have bought and companies they have dealt with, so marketers try to ensure that word of mouth is positive rather than negative. This is, of course, out of a marketer's control, but it is possible to influence it considerably and encourage it. For example, positive word of mouth is generated by bring-a-friend schemes, whereby someone who brings a friend along or encourages a friend to buy is rewarded in some way. In fact, these schemes work even better if the friend is the one who gets the reward – it is a chance for the customer to do a favour for a friend and is more likely to result in repeat business as the friend is the one who feels grateful.

■ **Word of mouse.** This is the online version of word of mouth and is also called viral marketing. Marketers put games or jokes online, with a hyperlink to send the URL to a friend. If the game is enough fun, or the joke is good (some companies use spoof advertisements for this), people will involve their friends in the joke or game. Sites such as Facebook, YouTube and Twitter have been used by firms, despite the general ban on commercial entries these sites have. Clearly, if a posting on YouTube is a well-made spoof advertisement, the moderators allow it to remain. Viral marketing should be distinguished from spam: spam involves introducing a computer virus which sends an advertising message to everyone in the individual's address book so that the message is sent (eventually) to an audience numbered in the millions.

■ **Product placement.** This means supplying products to film and TV companies to be used in the shows. At one time, producers were happy simply to be given the products to use as props, rather than have to go out and buy them, but the advantages of having a product appear and re-appear in a film, perhaps for many years as it is shown on TV, became so obvious that film companies now charge substantial fees for including branded products. In some cases, product placement deals are enough to fund a film entirely, and firms such as Coca Cola use product placement very extensively indeed.

EXAM TIP

If you are asked to make recommendations about a communications campaign, you should consider carefully the needs and likely behaviour of the target audience. For example, some products are better suited to mass advertising than are others, and some people are more likely to take an interest in advertising than are others. Professional people such as doctors or lawyers will be interested in anything which relates to their profession – doctors want to find out about new medicines, and lawyers want to find out about changes in the law or the regulation of the profession. This means that they will read their respective trade journals and will probably read the advertisements.

On the other hand, instant coffee (which is a mass-market item) should be advertised in a mass medium, using an advertisement which cuts through the clutter. It is quite certainly the case that mass advertising will cost a great deal more than tightly targeted advertising, so it is essential that you do not recommend such a course unless you know there is a mass audience.

The promotional mix is similar to the marketing mix in that one element cannot substitute for another, and each element acts on the others to create an overall effect. In recent years, the concept of integrated marketing communications has dominated academic thinking: the idea that all the messages emanating from the company should be essentially the same, no matter which route is chosen, is intended to ensure that there is no conflict between different messages or media. In practice, integration is hard to achieve because of the wide variety of possible messages and, of course, the wide variety of media involved: for example, sales people are likely to tell customers whatever they need to know in order to make a purchase decision rather than simply repeat the corporate story verbatim. Likewise, a message placed on the Internet has a different appeal and creates different perceptions from the same message placed in a specialist magazine or on a billboard.

ACTIVITY

Consider the last time you bought something from a salesperson (perhaps a shop assistant). To what extent did the salesperson discuss your personal needs? Were you asked about the uses you have for the product? Were you asked about how much you were expecting to spend? Did the salesperson seem interested in you?

If so, how did that make you feel? Would you be more or less likely to buy from someone who shows a genuine interest in your needs? Or would you prefer someone who just talks about the product?

MARKETING IN ACTION:
The Mini Cooper

In the late 1950s, a designer by the name of Alec Issigonis was commissioned to design a completely new car. At the time, there was a world oil shortage due to the Suez crisis, so the new car had to be small, cheap to buy and run, but roomy: it should also break the mould of previous car design. Issigonis came up with a revolutionary design – the Mini.

The Mini was one of the first production cars to have front-wheel drive and the first to have the engine mounted transversely rather than in a fore-and-aft configuration. This made the engine compartment rather tightly packed, but gave more room for the passengers – and the lack of a transmission hump gave more space in the passenger compartment. Issigonis even gave the car tiny 10-inch-diameter wheels so as to reduce the space taken up by wheel arches. The car was finally launched in August 1959, to a rapturous reception by the motoring press – the car was so revolutionary that people were hard-pressed to find anything ordinary in it.

During the 1960s, the car became a British icon. Despite some early teething troubles (the car leaked copiously whenever it rained and had an extremely lumpy gear change, for example), further versions were designed and snapped up by an eager public. Van versions, estate cars, convertibles and even the (supposedly) off-road Mini Moke were marketed. Issigonis said later, 'We made a car that was so unusual that it automatically became a status symbol.' Minis were seen everywhere and were owned by rich and poor, old and young: the car even featured prominently in the film, 'The Italian Job', starring Michael Caine and Noel Cowerd. Alec Issigonis was knighted by the Queen for his services to industry – a rare event for a humble industrial designer.

During the 1970s and 1980s, the car's fortunes slumped. Other small cars had entered the market, and poor quality of manufacture, frequent strikes at the factory and heavy competition from better-engineered Japanese cars caused sales to dwindle. Altogether, 5.5 million Minis were manufactured: many of them are still running, and in fact every part of the original Mini is still being manufactured somewhere to serve the army of Mini enthusiasts who keep these cars on the road.

Issigonis is quoted as saying, 'When I design my cars, they are styled so that they couldn't be obsolescent.' This has proved to be a telling statement. After BMW took over the Rover car company, it acquired the rights to the Mini design and decided that the car was due for a revival – updated, to a modern specification, with the 21st century safety features, but recognisably the Mini. For BMW, the problem shifted: they had to figure out the best way to cash in on the mini's iconic status!

At first, the Mini Cooper was launched in the United Kingdom, to great critical acclaim. The car was no longer the cheap runabout of the 1960s – but the baby boomers who had owned the originals were now in a position to pay the price to own a design classic. In addition, a new generation of Mini fans had been born.

For Rover, the key market to get into was the United States. With almost as many cars as people, the United States is the biggest car market in the world, and Rover intended to make inroads into it. The firm therefore hired US advertising agency Crispin Porter and Bogusky to run a $20 million campaign, with 25% of the spend going into print media. The objective of the campaign was to launch Mini into the United States by promoting it as an alternative culture called 'motoring' (as opposed to 'driving'). The British terminology helped to drive the campaign into becoming one of the most successful ever: the campaign won awards from Adweek and MPA Kelly, but more importantly it created such a demand for the car that long waiting lists appeared at dealers throughout the United States. The car itself won awards from consumer organisations, car journals and even the Kelley Blue Book (the car dealers' guide to used car values). In 2003, the car had a further boost in its fortunes when 'The Italian Job' was re-made using Mini Coopers as the getaway cars.

Mini even has its own website (common for a car manufacturer – unusual for a car) on which the themes of motoring, fuel economy and quirky originality are combined. The site is extremely interactive (it even tells users to get out in the sunshine more if they remain logged on for too long), and the site encourages visitors to 'e-mail a friend'. The website links to websites in other countries, each of which has a local character, but also conveys an air of Britishness. Each site includes an area where owners can join a Mini-owners club and can receive newsletters and special offers.

The overall aim is to recreate the sense of fun and uniqueness that characterised the first Mini, in the 1960s – and so far this seems to be paying off handsomely.

The Mini Cooper story shows us how a firm can integrate several communications media to generate a strong brand personality (or perhaps emphasise an existing brand personality). The agency, Crispin Porter and Bogusky, used the 'British' tag to create a novel and eye-catching campaign. Placing the product in 'The Italian Job' reinforced the brand values to the baby boomers who were the key target audience and also made great use of the Internet, playing to the strengths of the medium as well as conveying the message.

STUDY TIP

The promotional mix concept was first outlined in the late 1960s. There are many more tools available to marketers now, although the principle that the tools need to be combined in the right proportions remains. A full account of all the available tools is beyond the scope of this study guide, so you should read around your textbooks and other sources and familiarise yourself with the various tools.

You might also try observing marketing messages around you and categorising each one according to your list of tools – this will help you remember what they are and also give you some ideas, examples and templates to use in the examination.

CASE STUDY: Scotiabank

The Canadian banking system has, for many years, been an oligopoly – the major banks have controlled the market, and although regulation has been fairly tight, they have been able to set their own fees and service levels without too much risk of serious competition. As in most oligopolistic markets, however, the customer is the one who ends up losing out.

By the early part of the 21st century, banks in Canada had moved from being trusted custodians of the national finances to being regarded a necessary evil, monolithic enterprises with little regard for the customer's needs or well-being. Brand image advertising had made promises which never materialised, and banks were not differentiating themselves – banking had become a commodity and a disliked and mistrusted one at that.

Within this overall structure, Scotiabank decided to break the mould. The bank was at the time Canada's fourth largest – a position it had held since 1919 – and perhaps because of its relatively small size, it was regarded as a friendly, folksy bank. Its East Coast roots helped – Nova Scotia is often regarded as something of a rural backwater

in Canada, and Scotiabank was thought of as being somewhat unsophisticated, to put it kindly. This was no bad thing, given the developing climate of mistrust of banks.

The bank saw an opportunity to focus on four areas where management thought the bank could increase its market share:

1. Home lending. Scotiabank was losing market share, although mortgages were still big business for them: changes in the power of branch personnel to negotiate interest rates with customers were causing the bank to lose share.

2. Online activation. Scotiabank was falling behind other banks in online banking, a potentially serious failing since online banking cuts costs for banks as well as increasing customer service.

3. Small business. This represented a gap in the market, since none of the major banks had established itself as having capabilities in the small business loan market.

4. Investment. Research showed that few customers were prepared to consider Scotiabank for their

investment needs, and although this was not yet causing the bank any problems, it was clearly a ticking timebomb.

The bank had recently adopted a new core purpose, as follows:

'To be the best at helping customers to be financially better off by finding relevant solutions to meet their unique needs.'

The bank recognised that each of the markets it was aiming for had its own unique problems – but how were they to convey these effectively in an advertising campaign?

Scotiabank began by considering the unique aspects of each of the markets they wanted to enter. For home lending, they realised that buying the home was only the start of the financial problems – new homeowners need money for curtains, furnishings, legal fees, removal expenses and so forth, and may well have spent every last penny on the down payment. The bank therefore introduced cash-back mortgages. For online activation, the bank decided that customers needed a lot of help in learning how the systems could help them manage their cash better, without making trips to the bank to check on bank balances. For small businesses, the bank understood that business people are far too used to being rejected by banks. For investment, the problem for customers is not so much about understanding the worth of using their tax breaks to invest, but actually finding the money to invest.

In Scotiabank's research, one word kept coming up: respect. So the bank developed its creative platform on three principles: reflect the truth of customers' lives, be relevant to getting ahead financially (by offering a tangible Scotiabank solution), and reflect the customer's perspective, not the bank's.

The ensuing campaign used a problem–solution format. Each advertisement began by showing a common everyday financial problem, followed by the Scotiabank solution to that problem. The same format was used for television, print and radio advertising – for example, a businessman was shown leaving another bank, having been rejected for the umpteenth time and being offered a deal with Scotiabank through their ScotiaOne business loan package. ScotiaOne offers a single package for the small business, covering both personal and business banking, and also offers business advice.

The results? Over a 2-year period, Scotiabank increased its mortgage business by 13% ahead of the projected figures, it went from nowhere to being the industry leader in online banking in a period of only 3 months, it increased the number of credits in small business by 52% and experienced a 61% increase in dollar credits in small business, and it overachieved by 23% in recruiting new clients and overachieved by 11% in the investment business.

More importantly, compared with its rivals, it achieved the largest percentage awareness improvement of any Canadian bank, despite spending less than any of its competitors – another remarkable achievement, and one which can only have come about as a result of the advertising. In a market with very little differentiation, Scotiabank appears to have tapped into a real customer need – the need to be recognised as real people, not simply as account numbers.

Questions

1. How did Scotiabank translate its vision statement into an advertising campaign?

2. What sales promotion techniques did Scotiabank use?

3. How did the three principles translate into an integrated communications campaign?

4. What difficulties might there have been in offering a single, integrated message to such a wide range of potential customers?

Whether or not the marketing communications are integrated, it is certainly the case that each promotional tool will only work in specific circumstances, and yet each tool has an impact on the others. The coordinating mechanism must always be the brand image – what is the personality of the brand, and where do we want the brand to be positioned in the customers' minds? This is long-term, strategic thinking: we are trying to develop competitive advantage for the brand by careful use of communication.

For example, a money-off sales promotion might increase sales in the short term, but might damage the brand image by making it seem cheap and downmarket. In some cases, manufacturers have asked stores not to promote their brands in this way, for fear of doing damage to a brand which has been carefully positioned against its competitors as an upmarket brand. Equally, an advertisement might have an effect on a PR campaign (or vice versa – since both might appear in the same medium at the same time).

EXAM TIP

The promotional mix actually contains more than the four basic items – you will gain marks if you can 'think outside the box' and consider promotional methods which are unusual. You will also need to consider aspects such as the appropriate medium for your message: there is more on this later. You should, of course, link any recommendations to measurable objectives.

Keep in mind that, even though each element is taught as if it were a separate issue, you will be expected to consider all the elements as a whole (just as you did with the marketing mix as a whole). You will also need to distinguish carefully between the elements, in other words do not confuse advertising with PR (if you talk about 'free advertising', you mean PR or something else – advertising, by definition, is not free). Terminology is important in this, as in every other, profession: you need to be precise if colleagues (and examiners) are to understand precisely what you mean.

CASE STUDY:
Viral Marketing

Viral marketing has become one of the buzzwords of 21st century marketing. To many people, it sounds vaguely distasteful – connotations of virulent disease spring readily to mind, and it almost sounds like the worst kind of manipulation. In reality, it is simply a term for electronic word-of-mouth promotion.

Although viral marketing is not dependent on the Internet, it has become strongly linked with Internet marketing because e-mail is an extremely easy way to propagate messages. Offline, viral marketing is referred to as 'word of mouth', 'creating a buzz' or 'network marketing', but it is in fact the same thing – it is any strategy that encourages individuals to pass on a marketing message to others, creating an exponential growth in the message's exposure and influence. These messages are powerful, because they are credible: word from a friend is much more acceptable than word from a manufacturer.

The classic example of a successful viral strategy is MSN's Hotmail free e-mail service. Hotmail was one of the first free e-mail services on the Internet, and it owed its rapid growth to a very straightforward viral technique: firstly, the company gave away free e-mail addresses. Then, at the bottom of each message sent out by its users, it added the tag 'Get your private, free e-mail at http://www.hotmail.com'. This message was thus sent out to thousands more people, some of whom signed up for the service, and thus added to the number of people who propagated the name further.

Obviously, giving things away is not, in itself, a way to make money. However, Hotmail now has a large number of subscribers, each of whom is a target for buying other products from MSN. Every Hotmail subscriber sees several advertisements each time he or she logs on to send or receive messages, but this is a small price to pay for a free service.

To be effective, a viral strategy needs the following characteristics (Wilson 2000):

1. There should be a free gift attached.
2. The transfer to others should be effortless.
3. It should scale easily from very small to very large, in other words the system needs the capacity to start small, but handle very large numbers of people fairly quickly, otherwise it will drown in its own success.
4. It should exploit common motivators and behaviours.
5. It should utilise existing communications networks.
6. It should take advantage of others' resources.

The Hotmail example fulfils all of these criteria, as does Adobe Acrobat. The Adobe Acrobat Reader is free software: anybody who receives a PDF file from an Adobe subscriber can download Reader so as to be able to read the file. This has meant that Adobe Acrobat has become the leading software for creating and sending PDF files – which means that everyone who buys Reader is potentially a customer for Acrobat since they are able to see the quality of the documents that it produces. Acrobat, of course, is emphatically *not* free software. Annual turnover at Adobe is $1.2 billion, and the company has 3,700 employees worldwide – so viral marketing must have something going for it.

Viruses used in viral marketing are not the same as the malicious viruses which occasionally infect innocent computers. The essence of viral marketing is that the sender knowingly transmits the marketing message. In some cases, such as Hotmail, the sender transmits the message automatically every time he or she uses the service. In other cases, websites have a link (labelled 'Send this to a friend' or something similar) which encourages the individual to forward the entire website to a friend who might be interested. In order for this to happen, the website must contain something of interest – a free computer game, a free IQ test, some free software and so forth.

In some cases, viral marketing can use messages and imagery which would otherwise not be allowed in mass media – for example, the viral campaign for Trojan condoms developed by The Viral Factory uses some risqué images to get the message across. These images are likely to be passed on: other campaigns by the same agency are less risqué, but are equally engaging. In each case, they appeal to a particular target market, who are likely to pass them on to people with a similar sense of humour and similar interests.

Viral marketing also takes root in word-of-mouth campaigns. Word of mouth can be generated by allowing customers and others to take guided tours of facilities. A prime example of this is Cadbury World, a theme park outside Birmingham which is dedicated to the history of chocolate. Families and school parties are shown how chocolate is made and how the ancient Aztecs used chocolate, and even shown around a museum of chocolate-related artefacts. There are many other ways to generate word of mouth: the main element in generating word of mouth is to provide customers with something interesting to pass on to their friends.

The bottom line in viral marketing is credibility. People trust their friends far more than they trust a company – and they will listen to their friends far more than they will listen to an advertisement.

Case study questions

1. Advertising is heavily regulated: it must, by and large, be truthful. No such regulations exist on contacts between friends, so why is viral marketing more credible than advertising?
2. How might the power of word of mouth be transferred to advertising?
3. What type of organisation might benefit most from viral marketing on the Internet?
4. What other advertising media might be useful in driving customers to the website?

MEDIA DECISIONS

Choice of medium is as important as choice of tool, because the medium becomes part of the message. An advertisement placed in a cheap tabloid newspaper does not have the same message as the same advertisement placed in an upmarket broadsheet, and even TV advertising conveys different impressions according to the type of programme it is linked to.

Media can be assessed in several ways: the most basic is the cost per thousand, which means the amount it costs to reach a thousand people. This is not, in itself, sufficient: what is equally important is to ensure that the right people are targeted. Putting a message into the wrong medium simply means it will be ignored, because it will be going out to people who have no interest in the product: for example, a popular tabloid newspaper might have a high readership and an attractive cost per thousand, but most of the readers are likely to have relatively little education and small incomes, so advertising an expensive car would be futile. The same car could be promoted very well in a golfing magazine, however, since golfers tend to be better-off professionals.

The main media are as follows:

- **Television.** This medium requires the biggest budgets, but it also reaches the largest audiences. Until recently, targeting has been difficult because there were few commercial stations in the United Kingdom, but the advent of cable and satellite channels has provided at least some opportunity to target specialist audiences. Television advertising is costly but can have a low cost per thousand because of the very large viewing figures for some shows. It is most suitable for products with a very wide range of potential customers, for example, instant coffee or cleaning products.

- **Cinema.** This is often a neglected medium, but since cinema tends to reach a young audience, it can be very powerful, especially as it is difficult for the audience to avoid the advertising. Cinema audiences also tend to be wealthier and better educated than the average, so they represent a particularly desirable target audience for many products. The biggest advantage of advertising in cinemas, though, is that the audience are unlikely to ignore the advertisement. They are unable to switch channels as they would with TV, and they cannot get up and walk out while the advertisements are showing.

- **Billboards.** These are useful for localised campaigns, but are vulnerable to vandalism. Billboards are especially useful for retailers because locations close to the stores can be booked: billboard advertising can also be changed relatively quickly, since all that is needed is a new print of the poster and a man with a pot of paste and a ladder. For this reason, billboards tend to be used a lot during election campaigns.

- **Press.** This subdivides into mass media such as newspapers and popular magazines, and targeted media such as specialist hobby or trade magazines. Advertising in specialist hobby magazines is powerful because people are inclined to read the advertising: for example, someone who is a keen angler is likely to enjoy reading about new fishing lures in an angling magazine. Also, magazines are often kept for long periods (unlike newspapers).

- **Web advertising.** Pop-ups and banners can be powerful, but they can also be irritating for the audience. They do have the advantage of allowing interested consumers to respond immediately by being directed to an appropriate website. Weblinks are likely to be more effective, however, since many pop-ups will be blocked by the individual's firewall.

- **Radio.** This is often neglected as a medium, although it is cheap, flexible and difficult for the audience to avoid. It is often used as a reminder medium for TV advertising. People often listen to commercial radio while doing other things such as driving, housework, decorating and so forth, so they are often receptive to the advertising.

STUDY TIP

You will be expected to understand the relationship between the promotional mix tools and the media through which they operate, so it is a good idea to consider how various brand managers use the media to convey the different tools. Try looking at how a product's features and benefits are conveyed in a magazine as opposed to the TV, for example. Consider ways in which the medium affects the message.

CASE STUDY: Full Stop

This case study examines an integrated campaign for a charitable organisation (i.e. not-for-profit). The campaign used a wide range of media to convey messages to several different groups, each with a different angle on the same basic problem and each with differing needs.

In 2001, research conducted on behalf of the National Society for the Prevention of Cruelty to Children (NSPCC) showed that one in three people in Britain would not act to prevent a case of child abuse if they knew it was happening. The reason? They would not know what to do.

The NSPCC is over 100 years old. During that time, the charity has set out to protect children from all forms of abuse wherever and whenever it occurs – but without public support, they would have had no way of knowing that a particular child was suffering. The NSPCC relies on people calling in and reporting suspected cases – neighbours, teachers, parents of school friends and so forth. Since the charity was founded, other organisations have taken some of the burden of the work, however. Local authorities have Children's Services departments which investigate child abuse, the police have wide powers to act in child abuse cases, and other charities such as Action for Children and Childline (the emergency number which children can ring) have also contributed.

However, after discovering that many people would not know what to do if they knew a child was being abused, the NSPCC decided to run a major integrated marketing campaign aimed at stopping child abuse altogether. The campaign, called Full Stop, aimed to inform the general public about what to look for, and provided a telephone number (0808 800 5000) which people could call to report abuse.

The campaign included a series of TV advertisements using the Full Stop strapline, a billboard campaign featuring well-known personalities from the entertainment world, sport and politics, a radio campaign, a newspaper campaign and a website. Sponsored by Microsoft, the NSPCC campaign had four aims: first, to encourage people to report cases of child abuse; second, to encourage parents who might abuse their children to seek help when they feel that the stress is getting too great; third, to encourage children to talk about abusive situations in which they find themselves; and fourth, to raise funds for the charity. These aims were addressed at different times and using different advertisements, but the basic Full Stop message linked them all together. The campaign was backed up by a leafleting campaign and by a series of videos aimed at children and adolescents. Booklets distributed to schools, and an impressive website, have also dramatically increased the number of children who have come forward to report abuse.

One of the main outcomes of the campaign has been a huge increase in lobbying activities. Since the Full Stop campaign started, 140,000 people have come forward to help in the campaign, there is now a Children's Commissioner for Wales, 300 members of Parliament have signed the NSPCC Pledge on cruelty to children, and public awareness about child abuse has never been higher.

The NSPCC are realistic enough to know that child abuse will probably always happen. The fact that it could be prevented entirely if everyone worked together is undeniable, though, and the charity continues to work towards this ideal. Effective communication is a key plank in the platform for success.

Case study questions

1. What are the main communication factors which would prevent the NSPCC reaching its goal?

2. How might the NSPCC be more proactive in contacting potential abusers?

3. What other communications media might the NSPCC use?

4. What are the main problems for the NSPCC in producing an integrated campaign?

5. How might the NSPCC improve the integration of its campaign?

MEASURING THE SUCCESS OF PROMOTIONS

Although an in-depth study of market research is outside the scope of the Essentials course, it is useful to have some understanding of how promotional campaigns can be assessed.

Many non-marketers believe that the success of a promotional campaign can be measured in terms of sales, but in fact this is not true. For one thing, some tools such as public relations are not aimed at generating sales, but rather at generating goodwill and loyalty. For another thing, sales may be affected by many other factors such as competitive activity, Government initiatives or the general economic climate.

For these reasons, it is more effective to measure communications effectiveness in terms of communications outcomes such as brand awareness, positioning of the brand relative to competitors, knowledge of distribution and increased tendency to loyalty. This view of communications crystallised as the DAGMAR (Defining Advertising Goals, Measuring Advertising Results) model in the 1960s. The model implies that concrete, measurable communications objectives should be set for all advertising and the outcomes measured against these objectives. For example, an objective might be to raise brand awareness by 20% within 6 months: this objective is concrete and measurable, and is certainly a communications objective rather than a sales objective.

There are various techniques available for researching these issues, as follows:

1. **Questionnaire-type surveys.** These are usually problematical due to the difficulty of designing questionnaires which address the issues accurately and do not lead the respondents towards specific answers. However, they can be useful in assessing brand awareness. Brand awareness can be assessed either by using a prompted recall test (in which a list of brands is provided and the respondent is asked to state

which ones he or she recognises) or by an unprompted test (in which people are asked which brands in the product category they can remember, without being given any clues). Questionnaires can also be used to rank brands against competitors across various product attributes.

2. **In-depth interviews.** This technique involves asking people to talk about the brand and about the advertising in an open-ended way, with some guidance from the researcher. It is a technique which requires great skill from the researcher in not 'leading' the respondent, but it can yield a great deal of information, and has the advantage that the respondent may identify issues which the researcher was not aware were important.

3. **Focus groups.** This is a similar technique to the in-depth interview, except that the respondents are brought together as a group and invited to comment. This has the major advantage that the group members often spark off new discussion routes and can explore their ideas: since they often need to justify what they are saying to the group, the method compels them to think about what they are saying rather than simply telling the researcher what they think he or she wants to know. The danger with focus groups is that one or two members might sway the thinking of the others. Results are generally quick to obtain, and a large proportion of commercial market research is now conducted using focus groups since they appear to have better predictive value than questionnaire surveys. They are notoriously difficult to analyse, however.

4. **Sales patterns.** Although sales levels per se are generally a poor way to assess promotional success or failure, the pattern of sales can be indicative, provided it is used in conjunction with other methods. For example, repeat purchases can indicate greater loyalty, and surges in sales can indicate the success of sales promotions. Personal selling is almost always assessed in terms of sales volume, but seasonal factors can also be taken into account.

5. **Pre-testing.** Advertising can be pre-tested by showing the advertisement to a typical customer and assessing his or her responses. Focus groups are especially useful for pre-tests, but of course the test assumes that people will actually pay attention to the advertisement in the first place – it is much more difficult to test whether an advertisement is eye-catching or not. This can be checked using a portfolio test, in which a series of advertisements is shown and the respondent is asked which ones he or she can remember.

6. **Physiological measures.** This is a set of laboratory techniques in which individuals' responses are measured using such technology as eye cameras (which record the route an individual's eye takes when reading an advert), pupil dilation response (which measures the degree to which the person's pupils dilate when they see an advert – this is supposedly an indication of interest), and galvanic skin response by which the electrical resistance of the skin is measured (also considered to indicate interest).

SERVICES MARKETING

Virtually all products have some physical aspects and some service aspects. It would be a mistake to divide products into services and physical products, as if there were some definite dividing line between them. Having said that, some products have a much greater service element than others, and for convenience in writing we refer to these as service products. Service products have the following characteristics:

- **Inseparability of production from consumption.** In most cases, services are consumed at the time they are produced: one enjoys the meal while sitting in the restaurant, for example. There will be residual benefits in many cases: a haircut lasts for quite a long time after leaving the hairdressing salon, and a foreign trip continues after the airline has provided the transportation service.

- **Intangibility.** Services cannot be touched: the benefits are mainly in the mind and the emotions. Some aspects are tangible, of course, which is the physical evidence aspect of the marketing mix. Some services are less tangible than others, of course: an insurance policy is a great deal less tangible than a restaurant meal.

- **Variability.** Services are usually variable in that there may be differences from day to day, or from customer to customer. Sometimes the chef has a bad day (or a particularly inspired one), and of course a good hairdresser has to take account of the client's physical features and specific tastes. This means that each customer will come out of the salon with a different hairstyle from other clients.

- **Perishability.** Services cannot be stockpiled. Once an aircraft takes off, any unsold seats will remain empty and cannot be used the following day. Likewise, a hairdresser's time cannot be sold later – if client misses an appointment, the stylist can usually only sit down and wait for the next customer. This is a major problem for service industries, which is why many of them offer discounts or other incentives to fill quiet periods. Restaurants sometimes offer discounts to early-evening customers, and bars often run 'happy hours' where drinks are cheaper.

■ **Non-ownership.** Because services are intangible and perishable, the customer does not own them. In other words, there is no second-hand value for a service. There are one or two exceptions to this general rule: it is possible to sell an endowment insurance policy, for instance.

In markets where the service element predominates, there will be a greater emphasis on the final 3Ps of the marketing mix: people, process and physical evidence. People are usually taken to mean the 'front line' staff who deal directly with customers: the waitresses, truck drivers, receptionists, lawyers, accountants, hairstylists and so forth who deliver the service. Some commentators also include other people who may be present when the service is provided, that is, other customers. This can be an important factor – if we consider a restaurant, a bar or even a retail store, other customers affect the atmosphere and consequently our enjoyment of the service. An extreme case would be a nightclub, where the other customers are actually the product: most clubbers are not there for the music or the quality of the drinks, they go in order to meet other people.

MARKETING IN PRACTICE:
IKEA's co-workers

IKEA is a gigantic operation. The stores cover several acres, and each store employs 60 or more staff (called co-workers). The stores carry thousands of different products, and the whole experience can be so confusing for people who are shopping there for the first time that IKEA provides pencils, paper, tape measures and maps so that people can find their way around the vast stores and can make notes on what they want to purchase.

Inevitably some people become confused, disorientated, frustrated and error-prone in such an environment. Sometimes they will pick up the three-drawer model when they meant to pick up the four-drawer one, or they will get lost and wander in circles. Staff at IKEA are extremely well trained: they are cross-trained in sales and stock operations so that they can usually solve any customer problem, but more importantly they are trained to spot customers who are struggling or frustrated.

Co-workers are empowered to take a wide range of corrective actions. Apart from solving the immediate problem (being out of stock of an item, or helping the customer to find something) they can, when the situation requires it, offer customers a free meal in the IKEA on-site Swedish restaurant, or free delivery of an item, or cash coupons or even money off the purchase price of the product.

Over 200 million people visit IKEA stores in any one year – testimony to the effectiveness of the company's customer care policies.

As the case of IKEA shows, the people element in service provision can create competitive advantage. Empowering the workers to resolve problems instantly helps to create a positive working environment, but it also provides the customers with exemplary service–which is, of course, what service products are all about.

Physical evidence is the tangible aspect of service provision. The classic examples are the documents one receives from an insurance company as evidence of having a policy, the décor and ambience of restaurants and retail stores, and the tickets for airlines and railways. In many cases, physical evidence is used by consumers to help make a judgement about the likely quality of the service–a lawyer with a smart waiting room and luxurious offices gives an impression of success, which in turn inspires confidence in the client that the lawyer will be successful in fighting the case. Likewise, banks and insurance companies often have prestigious offices because this gives an impression of financial probity and solidity–important factors for financial services companies.

CASE STUDY: JD Wetherspoon

In 1979, law student Tim Martin decided he wanted to own a pub. Unlike most students with the same ambition, Martin actually went ahead and bought the pub he usually drank in. From the beginning, Martin decided that Wetherspoon's was going to be different from the other pubs around.

For one thing, Wetherspoon's has no music. There is no juke box, no live bands and no piped music anywhere in any Wetherspoon's pub. Second, Wetherspoon's has a wider range of beers than do most pubs–and it is the beer that makes the profits.

Wetherspoon's operate by keeping the price of the beer relatively low, but offering a quiet atmosphere, no-smoking areas and all-day food.

Each pub has its own name, but operates under the overall Wetherspoon brand: the pub name and the company name appear prominently on each of the 640 Wetherspoon pubs in Britain. The company was floated on the London Stock Exchange in 1992 and continues to expand throughout the United Kingdom. In recent years, the company has also diversified into J.D. Wetherspoon Lodges and

Lloyd's nightclubs. Each of these operations has the same philosophy as the central J.D. Wetherspoon brand.

Maintaining a pleasant, safe atmosphere is central to Wetherspoon's policies. The company has removed all financial incentives for customers to 'trade up' to larger or more alcoholic drinks: for example, most pubs sell a double measure of spirits for less than the cost of two separate singles, but Wetherspoon's have removed this because they see it as an incentive for customers to buy more alcohol than they otherwise might. Strange behaviour – most companies seek to encourage people to buy more of their products. The company also sell their soft drinks at much lower prices than most other pubs or restaurants.

John Hutson, managing director of Wetherspoon's, says, 'We believe that a combination of food served all day, reasonably priced soft drinks, an absence of financial incentives to 'trade up' to larger quantities of alcohol, combined with good facilities and a heavy emphasis on staff training are the right direction for the pub industry to take. . . . No company which serves alcohol can be immune from bad behaviour from time to time, but these policies should help to reduce its effects and, as a company, we will, as in the past, continue to consider sensible policies for our business and the community in this complex area.'

In another somewhat surprising development, Tim Martin called on the government to ban smoking in all pubs. Citing the Californian experience, where all smoking in public places was banned in the 1990s, he said that a significant number of people were avoiding pubs because of the smoky atmosphere. 'I believe that a total ban would be the best way forward, and not result, for example, in a situation where customers can smoke in pubs in Newcastle, but not in nearby Gateshead, because neighbouring councils have different agendas,' he said. 'However, it would be commercial suicide for a pub company to prohibit smoking in the absence of a nationwide ban by the government. Going it alone, in my opinion, is not a viable option in the pub world.' The government clearly took him seriously – smoking was finally banned in pubs throughout the United Kingdom in 2007. Some pubs have found that business dropped off, but many others have reported increases in business as non-smokers return.

The United Kingdom is a pub culture, like Ireland: much of Britain's social life revolves around drinking, and the corner pub is often the cornerstone of the community. What J.D. Wetherspoon has done is recapture the old atmosphere of the pub – a place for conversation, perhaps some food, and a comfortable and safe environment.

Questions

1. What is the role of physical evidence in Martin's thinking?
2. Why would Wetherspoon seek to have smoking banned in all pubs?
3. Why ban music in the pubs?
4. Why might Wetherspoon's seek to limit people's drinking?

ACTIVITY

Next time you visit a service organisation – a restaurant, store, bar, etc. – try listing the different things the management have done to create physical evidence. How have these elements combined to create a brand image?

Process is the series of events that takes place in order for the service to be delivered effectively. Even when the physical aspects of the service product are similar, the process can differentiate the products markedly: consider the difference between a hamburger from McDonald's and a hamburger from Hard Rock Café. Process can also change the dynamics of the service operation, reducing costs and increasing efficiency.

CASE STUDY: EasyJet

EasyJet, the low-cost, no-frills airline, has been the subject of many case studies and is widely used as an example of how an innovative approach to marketing can produce tremendous competitive advantage. This does not mean that things have always gone smoothly for the airline – in fact, at one point it looked as if the company was going to become a victim of its own success!

The demand for cheap flights, and the availability of new routes, was growing faster than the airline's ability to buy or lease aircraft. EasyJet could not afford to relax on opening up new routes, because a failure to seize opportunities in that regard would have left the routes open for competitors, of which many had grown up since the early days when Ryanair and EasyJet were the only two budget airlines in Europe. Also, passenger numbers were growing so fast that EasyJet's prices were rising – unless one booked very early indeed, the aircraft would be filling fast and the computer system would raise the air fare, thus destroying the company's main selling point.

The choices were simple: either the company would have to raise fares across the board and use the money to fund new aircraft (thus destroying the firm's only competitive advantage), or it would have to find ways to make the existing aircraft work harder. EasyJet chose the latter course.

Aircraft suffer from some limitations. They fly at the speed they fly: although it is possible to speed up a little, the cost in fuel outweighs the savings made. They have a fixed number of seats: unlike buses or trains, passengers cannot stand in the aisles. They cannot tow trailers, or have extra carriages put on, or in any way expand their capacity. Many airports nowadays do not operate on a 24-hour basis, because of environmental and noise considerations, so short-haul aircraft are effectively grounded overnight. The only slack in the system that EasyJet could identify was the turnround time on the ground: the less time spent on cleaning and servicing the aircraft ready for its next batch of passengers, the more time it could spend in the air.

EasyJet called in the consultants, but rather than hire time-and-motion consultants, the airline brought in a group which specialises in developing innovative corporate cultures. For the next 3 months the consultants interviewed all the people involved in turning round the aircraft – the baggage handlers, the caterers, refuelling companies, airport staff, EasyJet front-line staff, ground engineers, pilots, cabin crew and even the cleaning contractors. The consultants then were in a position to set up the right conditions for people who actually do the job to pool their ideas.

One of the early discoveries by the consultants was that people carrying out the various tasks did not understand how their processes fitted with other people's activities, because they had little or no idea of what the other teams actually did. Worse, they did not understand how each job was reliant on every other job. The consultants arranged for cross-disciplinary groups to meet and explain each others' jobs. The result of this was some creative ideas for cutting ground time. For example, ground engineers normally wait until all the passengers have disembarked before coming on board to discuss servicing needs with the pilots: this inevitably causes delays as it can take 10 minutes or more for passengers to collect their hand baggage and leave the plane. Discussions within the focus groups led to the idea of supplying ground engineers with headsets so that they can talk to the pilots from the tarmac while the passengers disembark, getting most questions out of the way before needing to board the aircraft. Another innovation is for the cabin crew to begin cleaning the cabin before the aircraft arrives – the cabin crew collect unwanted magazines and newspapers and any obvious rubbish while the aircraft is in its final approach and the seat belt sign is on.

Ideas were disseminated by videoing the sessions and allowing staff to see what the groups discussed. Ideas continue to flow from the staff, because they have developed an innovative culture. After all, who can understand the job better than those who do it all day, every day?

The net result of the exercise is that average turnround times are down from 50 to 33 minutes, and in one notable case an aircraft was turned round in only 7 minutes. This may not seem a lot, but if an aircraft makes an average of four return flights a day, over an hour per day will be saved in downtime. Over a working year, this equates to more than 60 return flights from Luton to Nice – which is equivalent to over a million pounds per aircraft in extra sales revenue.

Questions

1. How does the change in process affect EasyJet's unique selling proposition?

2. What might be the downside of the changes, from the viewpoint of passengers?

3. What effect do the process changes have on the firm's brand image?

4. What was the role of the people element in making the changes?

MEASURING THE SUCCESS OF MARKETING ACTIVITIES

Measuring success in marketing is not easy. Because much of what marketers do is concerned with establishing specific attitudes in consumers' minds, or with creating an image for a product, the difficulties inherent in assessing intangibles often result in no accurate assessment being undertaken.

Factors involved in measurement are as follows:

- **Budget measurement.** This is the degree to which marketing expenditures remain within the budget estimates. It is usually only relevant if the budget is based on sales turnover, but many firms do measure against budget, at least as part of the assessment of marketing success.

- **Objectives obtained.** Naturally, this relies on setting realistic objectives in the first place (see Unit 2). In some cases, objectives are easily measured: in other cases, for example, when trying to measure the success of a communications campaign, outcomes are difficult to measure. Communications activities can only be measured by communications outcomes – measuring by marketing outcomes such as increased sales is problematic since sales might have increased (or decreased) for any one of a great many reasons. If the objectives have been correctly set, using SMART (Specific, Measurable, Achievable, Realistic and Time-bound) as a checklist, the objective will be measurable.

- **Sales revenue, or profit and loss measurements.** The difficulty here is that many factors other than marketing activities can affect sales revenue, and even more is this the case with profit and loss. For example, a major economic downturn can wipe out sales, and at the same time a sudden fall in raw material prices or a currency fluctuation can make dramatic changes in profit and loss. These can easily mask any effects caused by marketing activities.

- **Efficiency and effectiveness.** Effectiveness is the degree to which something has worked and efficiency is the degree to which something has been achieved for a minimum of effort and expenditure. Each of these will involve other measurements (notably effectiveness) but they are useful as a way of understanding the impact of different marketing activities.

- **Level of defects or returns.** This appears at first sight to be an engineering issue, but in fact marketers need to be assured that goods going out to customers are fit for purpose. This is especially true in the case of services. Companies may aim for a zero-defect policy or in other cases expect a certain amount of complaining as being inherent to the business. If levels of complaints or returns are rising, the company may well want to do something about it.

- **Customer service complaints.** Two issues need to be addressed here: first, the level of complaints itself, as being indicative of customer dissatisfaction, or a mismatch between what the company provides and what the customers want, and second, the extent to which complaints are dealt with to the customer's satisfaction. Complaints which are satisfactorily dealt with tend to increase customer loyalty, which is why some firms actively encourage complaining.

- **Increased brand awareness.** This is usually measured by formal market research and is one measure of success in promotion. It does not necessarily translate into sales revenue outcomes, however – being aware of a brand is not the same as intending to buy it. Obviously increased awareness of the brand will probably increase the number of people who will be interested in buying, but in some cases people are aware of a brand in a negative way.

- **Changing attitudes.** Like brand awareness, this can be measured through good market research. Making changes in people's attitudes is one of the key functions of promotion activities, although in general attitudes tend to be stable and most promotion probably only acts as a reminder or 'nudges' people towards a purchase.

- **Repeat purchase and loyalty.** Some companies can measure this easily: many large retailers operate loyalty schemes, and many online retailers can track purchases. For other firms, especially those who are not close to the final consumers of their products, measuring repeat purchase and loyalty involves market research exercises.

CASE STUDY: Insight Express

Insight Express is a consultancy which specialises in online market research. Although the company's researchers are also experts in traditional approaches to marketing research, Insight Express has carved out a niche for itself in the collection and analysis of data obtained from Internet-based surveys and qualitative research. The company carries out research about advertising effectiveness, attitude and opinion evaluation, brand awareness and concept testing, customer satisfaction, market sizing, new product feature selection, price testing, and (in short) all aspects of consumer and customer research for marketers.

Insight Express say that the core of their success is the ability to deliver the online consumer and business audiences that match the clients' targeting criteria and are representative of the target markets. The company runs a panel called e-RDD which is their main pool of respondents, but has the capability to sample from up to 100 million online individuals. All respondents are 100% opt-in (they are all volunteers, in other words) and response rates run typically between 50 and 85%.

A recent research project carried out by Insight Express shows the power of their systems. In 2004, the company carried out an online survey on the topic of digital video recorders (DVRs) and found that 80% of respondents were already set up with a potential DVR device – their home PCs. Of these, two-thirds said they would be happy to use their PC as a DVR if it was easy and cheap to do so. This has major implications for electronics manufacturers (who may lose out badly), computer manufacturers and software companies (who will gain dramatically). The entire research programme was carried out within only 3 months – about one-third the time a comparable study would have taken by traditional methods.

Insight Express recruits its respondents by using pop-ups, pop-unders, banners, links and other call-to-action systems. Individuals who accept the offer complete an online screening survey which categorises them according to age, gender and other basic demographic attributes. Based on their answers, respondents are allocated to an active survey for which they qualify.

The company claims to have the sampling problem beaten because of the size of their population of potential respondents. In practice, there are some problems – although the Insight Express panel shows the same breakdown by gender and marital status as the population at large, their household income is (on average) 25% greater and the sample shows considerably fewer individuals in the lucrative 50+ age group.

For many types of survey, these differences do not matter: a representative sample can be drawn from the Insight Express population so that the overall results are more reliable. Whatever the arguments for and against online research, Insight Express have certainly found a potentially lucrative niche in the market research business.

Case study questions

1. How might Insight Express be able to help with assessing advertising effectiveness?

2. What type of marketing outcome would be reliably researched by Insight Express, and which would not?

3. Apart from sampling, what other problems might arise for Insight Express clients?

4. What factors might have biased the DVR research?

5. What problems might arise from using the panel approach?

EXAM TIP

You will be expected to be aware of the methods used for measurement and the ways in which they can be used, so you should be aware of the drawbacks and limitations of each. You should also consider if some are inappropriate with a marketing-orientated company.

Many students make the error of assuming that advertising can be measured by increased sales, for example, whereas advertising can only be measured by communications outcomes such as increased brand awareness or changed attitudes.

PUTTING IT ALL TOGETHER

You will need to be able to assemble all the elements of the marketing mix in order to make recommendations. Although the mix is dealt with as seven discrete factors, marketers (in practice) have to use all seven in the correct proportions and at the correct time to be successful. The coordinating mechanism is the brand personality, but the starting point for everything is the needs of the target customers.

In order to compete effectively, you will need to:

- Design a mix which is compatible and coordinated effectively.

- Think about your target market, their needs and expectations and also (of course) what the firm wants from them in return.

- Think about possible competitive responses. Competitors do not sit idly by and let you take their customers away – they will do something and it might be something serious.

- Think of the impact on the other elements of the mix if you start adjusting an element.

ACTIVITY

Here is a grid:

	Product	Price	Place	Promotion	People	Process	Physical evidence
Product	X						
Price		X					
Place			X				
Promotion				X			
People					X		
Process						X	
Physical evidence							X

Write in each box how you think the two elements might interact. This will help you remember the possible relationships. If it helps, you could consider them in the light of your own experiences in the firm you work for or any other marketing organisation with which you are familiar.

CASE STUDY: Manchester United Football Club

Manchester United Football Club (MUFC) exhibits an interesting difference over other football clubs. The vast majority of its fans have never seen the team play other than on television. This is because most of Manchester United's fans live outside the United Kingdom.

In 2002, fan club membership was spread across 200 branches in 24 countries. The Internet has enabled MUFC fans to communicate through chat rooms on every continent, including Antarctica – members of the British Antarctic Survey team often have to wait until the appropriate satellite is above the horizon in order to get the latest news of their team, but they feel it is worth the wait. The club even has its own TV channel – MUTV – available by subscription and pay-per-view. Even though membership of the US fan club cost $65 per person per annum, the membership lists had to be closed and the club's allocation of tickets (held in the New York State branch and available to members travelling to the United Kingdom) was over-subscribed by several hundred percent.

The huge international following for MUFC has opened up numerous possibilities for export marketing. A subsidiary company, Manchester United Merchandising, was formed to sell MUFC clothing, shoes, sports equipment, memorabilia and even telephone cards. In 1992, when the company started, the turnover was £2 million. By 1995, the turnover was £20 million and exceeded the gate receipts and programme sales for the entire year. By 2004, the turnover had grown to the point where playing football is merely a device for selling merchandise – the income from gate receipts is only a tiny proportion of the club's total income.

The monthly *Manchester United Magazine* spearheads the marketing effort, together with the bi-monthly *Manchester United on Video*. More than 140,000 copies of the English language version of the magazine are sold each month. The Thai edition sells 25,000 copies per month, and there are editions in Malay and Norwegian, with other foreign language editions to follow. The best markets for MUFC merchandise are Scandinavia, Ireland and Asia, regions where football is popular and watched extensively on TV and where there are strong national teams but few really big club sides. It followed from this that several other areas were ripe for targeting – the Middle East, for example – where the additional desirable criteria of a young population, high disposable income and the ability to watch matches on TV are also in evidence. South Africa is another target market for the club. The Manchester United brand is known worldwide, so the merchandising company is able to compete effectively with major sports equipment and clothing manufacturers such as Nike and Adidas.

Manchester United is in the early stages of internationalisation, however. MUFC still exports products directly rather than setting up local production or licensing arrangements. This provides the club with higher margins and total control over quality.

The vast majority of the club's income comes from its export markets – a far cry from the days when players were part-timers who had other jobs during the week, and the club's only income was the gate receipts.

Questions

1. Which elements of the marketing mix does Manchester United use, and in what ways?

2. What type of pricing strategy might be most appropriate for MUFC?

3. What effect would your choice of pricing strategy have on the MUFC brand?

4. Which promotional devices would be most appropriate for MUFC?

5. Why might MUFC have such a large following outside the United Kingdom?

SUMMARY

The marketing mix is a useful concept in that it brings together all the tactical tools that marketers have at their disposal and explains how each one affects the overall marketing effort. It should be used as a recipe: each ingredient, added at the right time and in the right quantity, contributes to the final result. It is important to remember that the elements all affect each other, and the total finished marketing plan will reflect all the elements.

It is also worth remembering that every firm supplies some services along with its physical products. These service elements (people, process and physical evidence) are often the only differentiators a firm has. One should also bear in mind that not everything fits neatly within the marketing mix 'silos' – like most models, it is for guidance and convenience of thought, it is not a prescriptive blueprint for action.

SELF-TEST QUESTIONS

1. What does PLC stand for?

    A Product-loving consumer

    B Product life cycle.

    C Product launch controller.

2. Which of the following is true?

    A Screening comes before idea generation, but after concept testing.

    B Concept testing comes after market testing, but before commercialisation.

    C Screening comes after idea generation and before concept testing.

3. Which of the following is true?

    A People can include other customers.

    B Product, for a retailer, means the products on the shelves.

    C Price is the only element of the mix which does not affect the other elements.

4. A new product which changes people's lives radically is called:

    A Continuous innovation.

    B Discontinuous innovation.

    C Dynamically continuous innovation.

5. Which of the following is true?

    A Early adopters buy after innovators, but before early majority.

    B Early majority buy before late majority, but after laggards.

    C Late majority buy after laggards, but before early majority.

6. Which of the following lists the elements of the traditional promotional mix?

    A Price, advertising, PR and personal selling.

    B Personal selling, advertising, PR and sales promotion.

    C Selling, advertising, sales promotion and personal communication.

7. Pitching the price low to start with in order to gain market share is called:

    A Penetration pricing.

    B Skimming.

    C Demand pricing.

8. Pitching the price high to start with then reducing it as competitors enter the market is called:

    A Skimming.

    B Penetration pricing.

    C Competitive pricing.

9. A firm which sells books on the Internet is an example of:

    A A wholesaler.

    B An agent.

    C A retailer.

10. The practice of moving goods through the distribution chain from raw materials to end user is called:

    A Physical distribution.

    B Logistics.

    C Marketing.

FURTHER READING

Since the marketing mix is such a large part of practical marketing, the reading tends also to be comprehensive. Chapter 1 of *Essentials of Marketing* (Blythe), plus chapters 6, 7, 8 and 9 for more detail on the mix elements.

Alternatively, Chapter 1 of *Principles of Marketing* (Blythe), with more detail in Chapters 12–22. Chapters 7–19 of *Principles of Marketing* (Brassington and Pettitt), Chapters 13–22 of *Principles of Marketing* (Kotler et al.), and Chapters 8–17 of *Principles and Practice of Marketing* (Jobber).

JOURNAL ARTICLES

Booms, B.H. and Bitner, M.J. (1982): Marketing strategies and organisation structures for service firms. In Donnelly, J.H. and George, W.R. (eds) Marketing of Services. (Chicago: American Marketing Association, pp. 47–52).

Levitt, T. (1986): The Marketing Imagination. (New York: Free Press).

WEBSITES

http://www.berr.gov.uk/index.html

The official website of the Department for Business Enterprise and Regulatory Reform. It contains a large number of articles and statistics on innovation, as well as advice for innovative businesses.

www.myoffers.co.uk

This website directs users to many sales promotions, providing a useful set of examples.

www.advertisingarchives.co.uk

This site contains advertisements going back over a hundred years.

This is an article about failed products, giving some of the reasons why they fail.

http://brand.blogs.com/mantra/2005/02/lovehate_brand_.html

This is a chat room for people to post their messages of love or hate about brands. It offers some interesting insights into what goes wrong with brand messages.

http://www.strangenewproducts.com

It is a website for weird and wonderful new products. The products themselves are genuine: some of them are definitely useful, others are useful but no one would buy them, and some are just plain crazy.

How to Pass the CIM Exams

The Chartered Institute of Marketing's (CIM) examinations are not a replacement for a degree course. They stand alongside, or even instead of, degree courses because the thrust of CIM thinking is towards the vocational rather than the academic. Degree courses tend to emphasise theory, and comparison of different models, whereas the CIM examiners are far more interested in your ability to apply what you know, in other words to think like a marketer.

This is by no means a minor distinction. Evidence from analysis of CIM papers shows that students who bring 'degree'-type thinking tend to do badly, whereas candidates who bring their marketing experience to bear do well. You should practise looking at every business situation (notably the case study in the exam) by asking the following questions:

- What can this company do immediately to improve the customer experience?

- What can this company do immediately to leverage its customer base into providing greater revenue and profits?

- How can this company differentiate itself from its competitors – in other words, what is this company able to do for customers which other companies cannot?

- Do my recommendations give someone a 'blueprint' for what they should do on Monday morning?

- Are the recommendations I am making worth somebody's money?

These are questions which you will be expected to answer in the real world: although (obviously) a CIM course is not the real world, CIM aim to make the exams as relevant to practice as it is possible to make them.

Thinking like a marketer means being a risk taker, being creative and innovative and using common sense – ask yourself whether you, as a customer, would react well to what the firm is doing. Marketers tend to think differently from other people in the organisation, if only because their focus is outside the organisation. Rather like someone who is choosing a Christmas present, marketers have to think like a customer, understanding his or her needs and wants, whereas the focus is internal for other people in the firm.

You should also bear in mind standard exam behaviour: if a question is only worth 4 marks, the examiner is only expecting a short answer. If a question is worth 20 marks, the examiner is expecting a much longer answer and you should spend the appropriate length of time on the question. You should also spend a few minutes just reading over the paper and ensuring that you understand the questions: sometimes candidates simply write down everything they know about (say) the product life cycle without actually answering the question (which may be about using appropriate communications tools at different life cycle stages and is therefore about marketing communications rather than the PLC itself). Remember that CIM examiners are not trying to trick you – they do not want to fail you, they want to grade you! There is a sample exam paper later in this section, with specimen answers of approximately the expected length, with comments on typical errors students make when answering the questions.

Here is a checklist for passing the exam:

- Read the paper and be sure you understand the questions. Many candidates are losing marks because they simply did not answer the question that was set. It is always worthwhile to spend the first 10 minutes or so of the exam reading the paper thoroughly.

- Work out how much time each question is worth and keep to that timing. If a question is only worth 4 marks, it should only be worth about 5 or 6 minutes of your time.

- Stick to the practical – do not just quote theory, use it to back up your recommendations. If you apply the theory, it will be obvious that you know it, so you do not necessarily need to repeat it.

- Ask yourself if your advice will improve the company's profitability or the customer experience, or preferably both!

■ Ask yourself if someone would be prepared to pay you for your advice. After all, that is exactly what you are expecting your current or future employer to do.

CASE STUDIES FROM PREVIOUS EXAMS

This section contains case studies from previous examinations, with an analysis of each. The most common errors made by students are also identified in each case.

MARKS AND SPENCER (DEC 2008)

Marks and Spencer (M&S) is a major UK retail chain, famous for its good-quality clothing and for exceptional food products. M&S is something of a UK institution – with 600 stores dotted throughout the country, and with many 'Simply Food' outlets on motorway services and railway stations catering to travellers, one is never far from an M&S store.

The company had its beginnings in 1884, when Michael Marks (a Russian-born Jewish refugee from the pogroms) opened a market stall in Leeds. Ten years later, he went into partnership with Tom Spencer, a former cashier: by this time, Marks had opened a store in Manchester and was beginning to expand throughout the North.

In the 1920s, M&S introduced the then-revolutionary policy of buying direct from manufacturers and registered their own label (St. Michael). Eventually (by 1957) all the products sold by M&S went out under the St. Michael brand. The company had a policy of buying British goods only and commissioned manufacturers to produce items to M&S designs and specifications.

The company had an extremely enlightened attitude to staff welfare, providing health care, subsidised canteens, hairdressing services and even holidays for staff – this was revolutionary stuff in the 1930s and ensured a committed and loyal workforce. In 1959 M&S banned smoking in all their stores (the first retailer to do so) and in 1961 banned all dogs except guide dogs, another first.

M&S have undergone several re-launches. The company's reputation for solid, serviceable, good-quality clothing has worked both for and against them – on the one hand, a reputation for clothes that will last is a plus, but on the other hand the same reputation can be perceived as a boring outlet for industrial-strength underwear. This tends to alienate younger shoppers. During the 1970s M&S re-designed the stores to create a 'younger' feel. During the 1990s the company had a major resurgence and was the first UK retailer to post profits of over £1 billion. The company dropped the St. Michael brand during this period, in favour of the 'Your M&S' brand.

The company's fortunes dipped again in the late 1990s, partly due to overpricing, partly due to the company's policy of not accepting credit cards (except their own) and partly due to the policy of only buying British goods. The company was simply unable to compete against rivals who were bringing in cheaper products from low-cost countries.

M&S now accepts credit cards and imports products globally, although they do insist on ethical dealings with overseas manufacturers. The company has a published code of practice for overseas suppliers which includes aspects such as workers' rights and working conditions.

Throughout the early years of the 21st century, M&S have worked to shed their somewhat dowdy image and attract a younger audience. Lively ad campaigns, new product ranges and store re-designs have all been aimed at re-vitalising the corporate image, while still retaining a degree of differentiation from other retailers. The 'Per Una' range of clothing has been introduced as a younger-looking line, while still retaining the reputation for quality for which M&S is famous.

In the longer term, M&S seems likely to continue to play to its strength, which is a reputation for high quality (albeit at a price). With its increased customer focus, this is almost certainly a winning formula.

Analysis

M&S is not an especially customer-centred company. They clearly put a strong emphasis on staff relations and (until recently) they obviously had a mission to support British manufacturing, even when this resulted in higher prices for customers. Again, until they were more or less forced to do it, the company did not accept credit cards, which for many British consumers represented a considerable inconvenience.

Stock policies also seemed to be less than customer-centred. Apart from the preponderance of own-brand goods, the company appears to have retained the same stock policies regardless of changing fashion, with the result that the company acquired a reputation for dowdy, old-fashioned clothing. Attempts to overcome this image (the Per Una range) have been difficult for the company, but they have made considerable strides in that direction.

The key issue with M&S, though, is its ethical stance. The company maintains exemplary working conditions for its staff and also tries to ensure that overseas workers are treated in a fair way: child labour and exploitative working practices are banned.

The company's pricing policy seems to be to charge a high price for top quality: this applies to both the food and the clothing ranges. This is a form of prestige pricing, especially for the food – the high price signals high quality.

COMMON ERRORS

The main area where students did badly on this exam paper was on the ethics question. Candidates often seemed to have difficulty in understanding what is meant by corporate ethics, or why it matters to marketers. The essence of the issue is that ethical companies acquire better reputations and are seen as reliable companies with whom to do business: regarding the staff welfare provisions, M&S are likely to have a much lower staff turnover and much more loyal staff – which is in itself a cost saving. In addition, the company is extremely unlikely to fall foul of legislation.

The other area where candidates did poorly was simply in not spending enough time on the questions. Often candidates would write only one or two pages – clearly inadequate for a question worth 20 marks. This is not to say that the answer needs to be four or five times as long as that for a 4-mark question: the examiners clearly expect that candidates will need to spend some time on analysing the case and thinking about their recommendations.

In some cases candidates described the theory they were applying in minute detail, which is definitely not necessary for the case study questions. Using the theory to back up the recommendations rather than describing the theory first is a far better approach.

LATCHWAYS (MAR 2009)

Latchways PLC is based in Devizes, Wiltshire, a rural area of England to the west of London. The company specialises in safety equipment for people who work at great heights, such as the outsides of office blocks, telecommunications towers, electricity pylons and so forth. The company was founded in 1974 and has patented systems for cable-based fall arrester equipment.

The heart of the company's product range is the Transfastener system. This allows workers to move freely as they carry out their work, without having to re-attach a safety line every few minutes: this avoids the possibility of human error when using a two-karabiner system in which the worker has to detach and re-locate one line while relying on another line, then detaching and moving the second line. Examples have occurred where workers have either accidentally detached both lines at once, or (because of having nowhere to attach the second line) have relied on only one line while working. There is also the problem of having to detach and re-attach lines while carrying tools or components. The Transfastener system avoids this scenario, since the worker only attaches the line once and can then work hands-free until the job is finished.

The system also incorporates a constant-force energy absorber so that (in the event of a fall) the worker is not jerked to a halt too suddenly, with a consequent risk of breaking bones or damaging internal organs. Latchways ensures that all its products conform to the Health and Safety Executive Code of Practice, which states (among other things) that:

> *It is the responsibility of the employer to ensure that any employee required to work at a height of 2 m or more must be suitably protected from any potential fall hazards. In the event of a fall the equipment used must be of sufficient strength to arrest a worker's fall.*

Since the company sells it products worldwide, it also needs to comply with foreign law, which differs from UK legislation in some respects. For example, French legislation specifies a height of 3 metres or more, Dutch legislation specifies a height of 2.5 metres and Spanish legislation specifies a height of 3.5 metres or more. In Spain, fall arrest systems such as those produced by Latchways are mandatory, but in France and Holland any system is acceptable provided it protects workers. In the United States, Latchways conform to the rigorous American National Standards Institute recommendations, which are tougher than the Government's Occupational Health and Safety Standards for Industry legislation.

Naturally, in an industry such as this quality is a major issue, so Latchways have devolved quality control to all employees. Each employee is responsible for maintaining quality and safety standards: rather than having a quality inspection at the end of the production process, each employee checks quality at every stage, thus maximising the chances of discovering any defects before the product is sold.

And the products do sell. Latchways has sold its ManSafe system to the Clifton Suspension Bridge, the Lysefjord Bridge in Norway and even the Sydney Harbour Bridge, where it is used to allow tourists to climb to the top of the bridge to enjoy the view over the harbour. St. Paul's Cathedral in London, Canterbury Cathedral and Portsmouth Dockyard all use ManSafe, and the company has even supplied the Royal Family – Buckingham Palace uses Latchways systems. Deutsche Telecom, Vodafone and NTL use the systems for ensuring worker safety when working on telephone masts.

Latchways has not been slow to expand the product range, either. In 2001, they incorporated HCL into the group. HCL is a specialist distributor of safety systems, providing Latchways with access to a wider range of customers. In 2004 the company acquired the rights to the Wingrip system, originally developed for aerospace applications but with potential for application elsewhere, and in 2007 the company introduced the Walksafe system for people working on roofs. As specialists in their field, Latchways also offers a free design and specification service so that contractors, architects and technical people can get the most from Latchways products. The company distributes its products through independent agents throughout the world, but places great importance on maintaining close relationships with its key account end-users.

So how is the company doing? In the 2007 Company Report, the directors reported a turnover of £31.9 million up 14% on the previous year. Earnings per share increased by 27%. Although the United Kingdom is still the company's main market, sales there grew by only 11% compared with 26% for the rest of Europe and a massive 97% for the rest of the world. Sales outside the United Kingdom now greatly exceed domestic sales, and as legislation is introduced in other countries (particularly in developing economies), the company expects to see even greater growth in future. Subsidiaries Safety Services (a specialist installation and consultancy arm of Latchways) and Specialist Fixing (the installation arm) both did extremely well. Latchways have directed some of the extra money towards research and development, doubling the size of the development team, and have also introduced a number of measures to increase efficiency as a way of offsetting some substantial increases in raw materials costs.

Overall, the future looks bright for the Latchways group. They are investing in the right places and they are in a business which can only see growth, partly as a result of more construction projects worldwide and partly because of a tightening of legislation.

Analysis

Latchways is a relatively small firm which operates in a global niche market. It therefore needs to understand trading conditions in those markets: although the basic problem which the company seeks to solve remains the same (all countries have a need for people to work at a height) the solutions need to be adapted somewhat to meet local legislation. Legislation is what drives Latchways: the tougher the regulations, the greater need there will be for the company's products, so the company needs to be aware of upcoming changes in legislation in order to be ready with a suitable solution. This is why the company has doubled the size of its development team in recent years and why its consultancy arm is doing well – customers need more help in understanding, and adapting to, the legislation.

The company empowers its staff to handle quality issues on the production line and adds value by offering consultancy services: although it is too small to have its own overseas sales offices, and therefore uses agents, the company takes a relationship marketing approach to its end-users. The company is therefore very marketing-orientated and expends considerable effort on understanding the markets in which it operates.

It is obvious that the global aspects of the company are going to take precedence in future. Growth in the United Kingdom is likely to be small as the market becomes saturated, so the focus will be overseas and the company will need to put more effort into understanding those markets. The company will also need to pay careful attention to distribution chain issues and may well need to increase its control over distributors.

Common errors

For this paper, relationship marketing was widely misunderstood – students really need to understand that this approach means taking active steps to retain customers with a high lifetime value. This goes beyond simply providing a good service or a good product: it means establishing a dialogue with customers, which Latchways seeks to do through its consultancy arm. The company should also do this through its website, which needs to be as interactive as possible and should have mechanisms in place for capturing information about visitors to the site.

It is entirely possible that some customers are not worth retaining, of course, and relationship market does contain this idea as well. This is why companies who want to take a relationship marketing approach collect information about all customers, not just those who seem particularly attractive.

Within the case study itself, some students had difficulty understanding the concept of adding customer value. All this means is that the company looks for ways to improve what they do for the customer, either without raising prices or by adding enough value to justify a price rise (as judged by the customer, of course). In the next question, candidates were asked to consider the effects of legislation on Latchways: many failed to recognise that increased legislation is helpful to the company, as it forces construction firms to adopt Latchways products. Too many gave the 'stock answer' that companies need to be aware of legislation which restricts their business – which is true, but which is not the key issue for Latchways. The final question for the case study concerned the 7P model of the marketing mix. Some students did no more than describe the 7Ps, without actually applying them to Latchways: others failed to recognise the importance of Latchways' design and development department, which is clearly an important service element.

Again, many candidates did not use their time well and some failed to use report format when asked to. This meant losing marks – you are expected to use the correct format in your working life, so you should use it when asked to in the exam. Up to 10 marks are given for using the correct format.

APPLE AND THE IPHONE (JUN 2009)

In January 2007, Apple Corporation unveiled its latest must-have gadget: the iPhone. Building on the success of the iPod music system, the iPhone is a mobile telephone with all the bells and whistles. It connects to the Internet, it has a 2 megapixel camera, it will store up to 1,000 songs, it has a screen three and a half inches wide (big enough for TV shows), it will do everything the iPod does and it will also make telephone calls. And what telephone calls! Apart from the usual address book and automatic dialling that every-one expects from a mobile telephone, the iPhone can hold calls while the user answers another call, and can even set up a conference call. There is no keypad – everything is controlled from the touch-sensitive screen. Basically, the iPhone does everything any other telephone in the world does and it connects to the Internet. Apple launched the product in the United States in January 2007, intending to roll the product out worldwide over the ensuing 12 months or so, in order to manage demand.

Demand has been strong. In April 2008, the company reported that they were unable to manufacture the telephones fast enough to meet demand, despite the £500 price tag in the United States. Part of the problem was that enterprising Nigerians were buying the phones in New York in lots of 500 and shipping them to Nigeria where demand among wealthy Nigerians was taking off – Apple's careful worldwide roll-out was being undermined within days of the launch, partly as a result of the weak dollar. People used to paying $500 for a Blackberry were delighted to find they could buy an iPhone for a similar amount.

The launch was not without other problems. Cisco Systems filed a lawsuit alleging trademark infringement within hours of the launch: Cisco had launched an Internet-enabled telephone in 2006 under the name iPhone, but were prepared to share the name provided certain conditions were met. They alleged that Apple went ahead with the launch before the discussions were concluded, whereas Apple claimed that the talks were almost finished apart from minor details. This wrangling over the brand name did not affect Apple's shares – they soared on the launch of the iPhone. In any case, Apple is no stranger to lawsuits – they have even been involved in a long-running legal battle with the Beatles, whose own record label is also called Apple and uses a similar logo.

Apple has, according to business analysts JD Power, the highest rate of customer loyalty of any computer/electronics manufacturer. Apple operate their own network of retail stores and each new opening is usually marked by huge crowds waiting to be the first to see the latest gadgets (in Tokyo, the queue stretched for eight city blocks). Apple's consumer base is reputed to be unusually artistic, creative and well-educated: the company has fostered this image, using advertising which reflects a rebellious image.

Certainly the iPhone proved popular when it was finally launched in Europe. O2, the telephone service provider, secured exclusive rights to sell the iPhone: they reported selling tens of thousands of the units in the first weekend of the launch. Germany's T-Mobile sold 10,000 units in the first afternoon of the launch and O2 went on to sell 200,000 units over the Christmas and New Year period. Apple have tried as far as possible to distribute via network operators, linking the telephone to contracts.

Not surprisingly, the major players in the world's mobile telephone industry were quick to respond to this entry by a new competitor. Nokia's N95, Sony-Ericsson's W960, Samsung Blackjack and several others were already regarded as serious competition, but the majors are working to develop similar touch-sensitive screens and interfacing in order to meet the threat head-on. The relatively high price of the iPhone (around £300 if the buyer takes out an 18-month contract or €799 in Germany without a contract) means that competitors have some scope for undercutting the price. Apple would almost certainly be in a position to retaliate, however, since the colossal sales figures so far have almost certainly meant that the company will have covered the development costs of the iPhone and can afford to move the price closer to the costs of production. Meanwhile, Vodafone ran a specific feature on its website offering 'alternatives to iPhone', at lower prices – possibly a somewhat desperate measure, given that Vodafone were thus giving the impression that the iPhone was a better product!

In the longer term, there is little doubt that competitors will erode Apple's lead in the market. Whether Apple can maintain their position by bringing out an even more advanced and exciting model remains to be seen – but there is little doubt that the iPhone has generated a great deal of consternation among the established firms in the mobile telephone business.

Analysis

This case is largely about new product adoption, but it also contains elements of pricing. Apple tried to roll out the launch of the iPhone globally by launching sequentially into different markets. This was probably because they could not manufacture the phones in sufficient quantities for a global launch, and in any case would not have had the necessary resources to promote, deliver and service that many phones all at once. The gradual roll-out gave competitors a chance to respond, though.

The price-skimming approach which is evident in Apple's behaviour probably helped to mitigate the effects of the global roll-out, since it should have limited the grey market – unfortunately, this did not work very well, since Nigerian entrepreneurs bought up large numbers of the iPhones to ship to West Africa: the weak dollar helped this process along, of course.

Apple is not displaying the marketing concept here. It is, in fact, a product-orientated company, making something which has all the features that anyone could want, and thus having to charge a very high price indeed as compared with other mobile telephones. Surprisingly for marketing theorists, this seems to have worked very well – despite the complexity of the product, sales have been excellent. This may in part be due to Apple's customer base, which is supposedly more creative, artistic and educated than the average – this is not surprise, given the price of the phone, since it can only be afforded by well-off people.

Common errors

Many students became sidetracked into telling us everything they knew about the iPhone rather than keeping to the marketing aspects. Others suggested that Apple should have continued with the global roll out without thinking through the possible reasons why the company could not have done this: many others thought the price skimming idea was bad, in view of the fact that competitors quickly entered the market. In fact, price skimming (or indeed prestige pricing) is the ideal way to price such a product, since it has great appeal to innovators. Few, if any, students picked up that the company is not customer-centred but is in fact following a product orientation.

The first question for Part B asked candidates to identify what Apple might have learned from the launch. This was a straightforward question about the candidates' analysis of the case, yet many candidates had trouble identifying that Apple underestimated the demand for the product and also that the company did not have systems in place to prevent people from buying large numbers of the phones. The second question asked candidates to identify potential threats from competitors: some failed to see that competitors might enter markets that Apple had not yet got round to, notably the Nigerian market where people were prepared to pay a premium price over and above Apple's already high price in order to get their hands on the iPhone.

The final question for Part B asked candidates to explain the iPhone pricing structure. In fact, the pricing structure is perfectly reasonable for the type of product, but many candidates suggested lowering the price in order to shut out competition or (bizarrely) using penetration pricing to capture a large part of the market. In circumstances where the company could not manufacture the phones fast enough to meet demand at a high price, it is difficult to see how dropping the price dramatically would help.

ALLIANCE BOOTS (SEPT 2009)

Background

Boots the Chemist is a well-known brand name in the United Kingdom and throughout the world. The company merged with Alliance Unichem plc in July 2006 to create Alliance Boots plc. The combination of Boots' strength on the High Street and Alliance Unichem's strengths in wholesale and distribution are seen as important elements for the company's success.

Mission

Alliance Boots' mission is 'to become the world's leading pharmacy-led health and beauty group'.

We will seek to develop our core businesses of retail pharmacy and wholesale across the world and become a significant player in many major international markets. Performance-driven, we aim to set high standards that are recognised as the benchmark by all our stakeholders, including employees, manufacturers, pharmacists, consumers and payers. We intend that our brand portfolio will lead the industry and we aim to demonstrate unparalleled expertise in formulating, marketing, selling and distributing our own brands. We will create a strong shared culture and sense of identity and belonging for our team throughout the Group.

Channels

Following the merger Alliance Boots has over 3,000 pharmacies: 2,550 stores in the United Kingdom and 500 overseas stores in Norway, Thailand, Ireland, Italy and Switzerland, as well as wholesale outlets in 14 countries. The company's branded products sell in many other countries, including the UAE, United States, Kuwait, Qatar, Russia, China, Spain, Canada and France. In addition, Boots' Wellbeing website offers thousands of products online, with free delivery throughout the United Kingdom on orders over £40.

Most stores are located on high streets, but in line with modern shopping trends, Boots the company is rapidly increasing its presence in out-of-town retail parks, where 48 new stores have been opened in the last 3 years. At one time, it was estimated that 40% of the women in the United Kingdom would visit a Boots pharmacy in any one week.

Product range

The largest part of Alliance Boots' business is prescription dispensing and consumer healthcare. There are pharmacies in almost all of the stores, with over 100 million items being dispensed each year. An increasingly important part of the dispensing business is the Prescription Collection Service, which accounts for about one third of all items dispensed in store. The company also has the largest UK share of the over the counter medicines (i.e. those that can be sold without a prescription).

The group sells more than just medicines, of course – it has its own beauty product ranges and also sells products for babies, suntan lotions, cooking utensils, cameras, some electrical goods, some books and gifts. Its own brand and exclusive products account for around 35% of the company's total sales and, in addition, Boots' No7 cosmetics range remains the UK's biggest selling cosmetics brand by revenue.

Corporate social responsibility (CSR)

Alliance Boots views the key to the successful introduction of its new group-wide CSR strategy as the recognition that operating units in different countries face different challenges. The company has devised a new support structure that will help it to develop and take ownership of CSR programmes that are appropriate to local circumstances, while remaining within a consistent Alliance Boots framework.

Each country will appoint a senior director, with overall responsibility for CSR and for delivering against locally set targets. Because of the importance the company attaches to developing CSR, each of those directors will also act as the country champion, responsible for the day-to-day running of CSR activities. Support and additional expertise will be available from a member of the CSR management team. An in-country advisory body will provide further guidance and an independent view of local priorities and sources of advice and funding within the country in question.

The aim of the CSR programme is to grow a more sustainable company in the community by focusing on the following areas:

- community
- environment
- marketplace and
- workplace.

The company has set four particular priorities, comprising the following:

- community health care
- carbon management
- stewardship and integrity of products and services, and
- employee well-being.

Alliance Boots believes that running a successful business and providing a socially valuable service go hand in hand. The company's press office issues regular press releases, emphasising the company's corporate social responsibility credentials; in general, these are very strong, the Boots brand in particular being a well-trusted name. Corporate initiatives include sponsoring a new degree in international pharmacy (run jointly by the universities of Nottingham in the United Kingdom and Tor Vergata in Italy) and increased investment in local community pharmacies. The company continually seeks greater efficiency in the supply chain in order to maintain lower prices for customers.

Market growth

In February 2008, Alliance Boots announced a new joint venture taking the company into China. The company is joining with Guangzhou Pharmaceutical to acquire a major footprint in China, hoping to gain a substantial share of the market. Meanwhile, Boots has retreated from Hong Kong, handing over its interests in the former British colony to Hutchison Whampoa's Watsons chain of pharmacies.

China is the ninth largest pharmaceutical market in the world and is experiencing rapid economic growth across the economy, and in health care expenditure in particular. It is estimated that by 2010, China will have become the sixth largest pharmaceuticals market.

Analysis

Alliance Boots appears to be practising societal marketing. Its mission statement and its very extensive corporate social responsibility programme show that the company is dedicated to the idea of being a leading corporate citizen by sponsoring universities, community healthcare, carbon management, integrity of products and services and employee welfare. The mission statement is clear about looking after the interests of all stakeholders, with consumers coming well down the list. This mission statement implies a strong emphasis on PR, on internal marketing initiatives, on moving into global markets and on staying with pharmacy as the core business rather than venturing off into other retail functions. The intention to be performance driven implies tight management objectives and good control systems.

The mission statement drives the organisation: everything the company does stems from this. It operates in many countries and has a policy of thinking global and acting local – local managers have a great deal of autonomy in running the business, especially the CSR aspects, so the mission statement needs to be interpreted in each market in which the company operates.

Common errors

Many students struggled with Question 11, which asked them to explain how Alliance Boots' mission statement could be translated into solid tactical actions. Several discussed SMART without actually recommending any objectives and most missed the importance of CSR to Alliance Boots, even though this was flagged up as being extremely important to the company. Question 12 asked candidates to suggest communications methods for flagging up the CSR programme with various stakeholders. This went better: candidates recognised the role of PR and internal marketing and were able to come up with tools for achieving the required outcome.

Question 13 was about adapting the marketing mix for the Chinese market. Several candidates only considered the people, process and physical evidence – nothing about the other four Ps. The extended marketing mix (7Pmodel) includes the original 4Ps and should be considered as well. Unfortunately, many candidates confined themselves to describing the elements of the mix without actually applying it to the Chinese situation and explaining how the mix might need to be adapted. Overall, this lack of applying the theory to a real situation was the downfall of many students.

Many students failed to use report format. This lost marks unnecessarily – report format is simple to apply and should be used when required in the question.

GLAXOSMITHKLINE (DEC 2009)

GlaxoSmithKline (GSK) was formed in 2001 by the merger of Glaxo Wellcome (itself a merger of Burroughs Wellcome & Company and Glaxo Laboratories) and SmithKline Beecham (created from Beecham and SmithKline Beckman). The company is the second largest pharmaceutical manufacturer in the world, based on sales volume. The company produces both over-the-counter medicines such as Panadol (a paracetamol-based pain killer) and prescription drugs such as Flixonase, a steroid-based nasal spray used to treat hay fever and other nasal inflammations. Many household medicines are

GSK products: Niquitin tablets (which helps smokers to stop smoking) and Lucozade (an energy drink) are both produced by the company.

From a marketing viewpoint, pharmaceuticals represent an interesting challenge. Prescription medicines (known in the trade as ethical medicines) cannot be sold directly to patients and doctors do not themselves buy them. Pharmacists will only stock medicines that doctors will prescribe, so the main thrust of the manufacturers' marketing effort is geared towards persuading doctors to prescribe the medicines to appropriate patients. From a doctor's viewpoint, this is only likely to happen if the new medicine has significant advantages over the ones it replaces, so there is strong pressure on pharmaceutical manufacturers to innovate.

In consumer markets, there is somewhat less pressure to innovate, but as medical science progresses more products will come onto the market anyway. The problem here, as with ethical medicines, is that each new product must pass strict tests before it can be launched onto the market – drugs also have to be tested in several different countries against different medical criteria. No drug is perfectly safe and a drug might be turned down in one market and passed in several others.

In order to maintain the flow of innovation, GSK has a continuous 'development pipeline' for new ideas. The company has Centres of Excellence of Drug Discovery (CEDDs) which are focused on five therapeutic areas:

1. *Infectious diseases*. These are diseases carried from one person to another by micro-organisms such as bacteria and viruses.

2. *Metabolic pathways*. These are diseases caused by malfunctions in the patient's body, such as diabetes or thyroid deficiency.

3. *Neurosciences*. These are diseases of the nervous system.

4. *Respiratory ailments*. The respiratory system is anything to do with lungs, throat and nasal passages.

5. *Immunoinflammation*. This is the area of pain relief and anti-inflammatory medicines.

During 2007 the company invested £3.2 billion in research and development: it takes between 12 and 15 years to develop a new drug from first discovery to marketing, due to the strict testing before a drug is approved for use. A typical new drug will cost around £500 million to develop. Not all the research is carried out in-house: GSK sponsors research in universities as well, much of which is 'pure' research, that is research for which there is currently no known use. Pure research is simply a quest for knowledge and the company finds it worthwhile to sponsor this because it is where many of the best ideas come from.

Eventually, research needs to be carried out with human subjects, at which point volunteers are needed. The drugs will already have been tested extensively on animals. Provided no serious side-effects are detected, the drug can go for clinical trials to be tested on a group of people suffering from the disease to see whether the drug helps. With this type of testing, another group of patients will be given either a different drug or a placebo (a fake medicine which has no effect) to ensure that the effects of the drug are not confused with some other factor.

The company clearly has a series of ethical challenges to deal with. Use of animals in experiments is one – currently, the company seeks to minimise the use of animals, especially 'higher' animals such as dogs or monkeys. Another issue is the clinical tests, in which some patients will not be given the new drug while others are – if the drug is effective, the ones without it are being refused something that might save their lives.

Ultimately, the pharmaceutical industry is one which is risky: marketing a drug that turns out to have serious side-effects could mean paying out billions in compensation. Equally, millions could be spent on research that bears no fruit. Furthermore, there is the marketing risk – the new drug may not be significantly better than what is already out there or a competitor may produce something that works better while testing procedures are being implemented. On the plus side, a successful new drug will make billions – it is a global market, and once established, a drug can produce income until the patent expires.

Analysis

This case is largely about the problems of operating in a high-risk, high-return industry. GSK is a global corporation operating in a volatile market – at any moment, another manufacturer might develop a drug which will out-compete GSK. The key issues here are new product development and port-folio management: there are unlikely to be as many problems in adopting a new drug, since a successful cure for a disease will find a market provided the missionary salespeople do their job in persuading doctors to prescribe the drug. New product development is very long drawn out because of the need for rigorous testing and it is also expensive because it requires the efforts of highly skilled (and highly paid) scientists. Protecting intellectual property is important to pharmaceutical companies.

Distribution is an issue, because some drugs are only available on prescription and the rules for this vary from one country to another: distribution has two meanings, one being concerned with place issues such as which retail outlets or pharmacists can be targeted and the other having to do with the logistical aspects of getting products to the right location. The logistical aspects are complex because drugs are valuable, often perishable and are also often a target for thieves.

The company also faces ethical problems, not least because of the need to test new drugs, often on animals, before releasing them onto the market.

Marketing of new prescription drugs is likely to involve missionary selling since the doctors decide what to prescribe, but do not themselves buy drugs in any quantities. In many countries, it is illegal to advertise prescription drugs to the general public. Pharmacists will only stock drugs which are prescribed and over-the-counter medicines. GSK's sponsorship of universities is only partly a PR exercise: it also generates ideas and processes which the company can use commercially. The company already owns several well-established brands in the general 'health care' category and could build on this aspect of their activities.

Common errors

Students often failed to discuss both aspects of the distribution question, sometimes concentrating entirely on logistics and sometimes concentrating solely on place issues. Few students managed to consider these aspects in a global context. Portfolio management also proved problematic: students were able to outline the product life cycle and portfolio management models (such as the BCG matrix) but were unable to recommend ways of extending the company's brands (e.g. Lucozade or Niquitin). Students seemed unable to place GSK products on a continuum in terms of their position on the PLC or the BCG matrix.

On Question 13 (which asked students to recommend communications tools for communicating with health professionals), many students simply described several communications tools, without applying them directly to GSK or the pharmaceutical industry. In some cases, students suggested inappropriate approaches, such as mass media advertising of prescription drugs: this is clearly a wasteful thing to do, since doctors are a small proportion of the population, and in any case it is illegal to advertise prescription drugs in many countries, including the United Kingdom. In general, the section on assessing the effectiveness of communications (which was the second part of Question 13) was well answered, although many students did not relate their answers directly to GSK.

Some students repeated large parts of the case study, explaining the history of the company despite the fact that they were (supposedly) writing a report for the boss, who would presumably know at least as much about the company's history as the student would. This simply wasted time and paper. Overall, there was often a failure to relate answers to the case study – recommendations must relate to the circumstances of the case or they are worthless to the company.

SUMMARY

The basic problem with answer papers is students' failure to apply the theory. This may stem from a failure to analyse the case study adequately: it is wise to spend some time thinking about the implications of the case rather than simply read it through and then seek to answer the questions. Broadly speaking, candidates have tended to talk about the theory far more than is necessary, without showing how it is relevant to the case itself: after all, you are supposed to be writing a report with recommendations for your boss, who is likely to know the theory already.

You should practice analysing cases – there are several in this study guide for you to start on – and think about the answers you are giving. Imagine what it would be like to be working for those companies and actually having to come up with recommendations for expanding the business. You might also watch the business press and see how companies solve their problems. Visiting company websites can also provide insights – obviously firms are unlikely to publish sensitive corporate information on their websites, but many firms provide their annual shareholders' report and these can often be instructive since the companies concerned are eager to boast of their successes.

Sometimes students lost marks through not using report format when asked to. You are expected to understand and use report format sometimes – this is a business skill which is widely used and certainly if you work in a larger firm, or work as a marketing consultant, you will need to understand and use it.

Having said all that, many candidates do answer the papers well and consequently obtain good grades. Even more answer most questions well, with some errors, and consequently pass the exam.

SAMPLE SHORT QUESTIONS

This section should help you to answer the short, 4-mark questions in the paper. Many candidates tend to write too much or simply 'brain dump' the theory they know into the paper, whereas candidates who gain distinctions will use examples and apply their knowledge.

The following questions are typical of those you are likely to find in the paper you sit. Each one has a sample answer attached to it and a description of some of the problems candidates have had in answering this type of question. Note that the answers are short – you might like to try writing them out by hand, to see how long it takes you. Each answer should take you around 3–4 minutes to write out, but you are actually given around 7 minutes in the exam to do this. The CIM is not testing you on how fast you can write by hand, after all!

TASK ONE

Explain how marketing orientation will help stakeholders of a charity.

(4 marks)

Specimen answer: *For charities, the concept of meeting customer need extends to all stakeholders: contributors, beneficiaries, volunteer and paid staff. The needs of contributors might be to feel that their money is going to be put to good use and also to feel good about contributing: a charity should acknowledge the contribution in some way. Beneficiaries need to feel that the help is appropriate and they should also be treated with respect, not as freeloaders. Volunteers need to feel valued and also often have social needs – friendship, a place in the community and so forth. Paid staff need to feel that they are working for a good cause and should be helped to 'buy into' the charity's aims, with good internal marketing initiatives. The charity might have some difficulty in reconciling the different needs of these various stakeholders.*

For this question, the key point is that charities have stakeholders rather than customers, and therefore have a somewhat different perspective on meeting needs. You would be expected to be able to identify at least some of the stakeholders and their needs, and be able to explain the role of marketing orientation in meeting those needs.

TASK TWO

Explain, with examples, what is meant by the maturity and decline stages in the product life cycle.

(4 marks)

Specimen answer: *Maturity is the stage when a product's sales are stable, the brand is well-known and the company need only spend money on reminder advertising rather than on building awareness. An example would be Marmite, which has been around for many years, is widely available and requires relatively little advertising. The decline stage is the point at which a product's sales are falling, its market is diminishing and eventually the product will disappear altogether. An example might be landline telephones, which are gradually being replaced by mobile telephones and may well disappear within the next 20 years or so.*

In some cases, students get distracted into writing down everything they know about the product life cycle, with a diagram as well. The question actually does not ask for this, but it does ask for examples: you will lose marks if you cannot put examples in.

TASK THREE

Describe how marketers in a business-to-business (B2B) organisation might go about setting marketing objectives.

(4 marks)

Specimen answer: *The marketers will begin with the corporate objectives laid down by the directors of the firm. They should then conduct a marketing audit to see where the firm is now, then set objectives which will move the firm from its current position to where it wants to be. In a B2B context, objectives need to take account of the long-term relationships the firm has or wants to develop with its customers and suppliers, so this part of the marketing audit will be especially relevant. This is the marketing strategy, which can then be expressed in terms of tactics, implementation and monitoring, and control. Objectives should be specific, measurable, achievable, realistic and timebound.*

In some cases, candidates have been known to start writing all about B2B marketing rather than describing how objectives are set.

TASK FOUR

Explain how communications technology can be used to develop and maintain effective relationships with distribution channels.

(**4 marks**)

Specimen answer: *Establishing and maintaining relationships depends heavily on good communications. Firms can use the database to ensure accurate communications with the right people and should be using e-mail for regular communications with appropriate individuals within the distribution companies. Direct links between the companies' computer systems can make stock checking and shipments much more efficient, which will in turn tend to 'lock in' the other companies. An interactive website will help in making information flow more easily and should help in identifying the needs of the distribution companies as well as flagging up more efficient ways of working together. Linking front-line staff such as delivery drivers and order-chasers through SMS or mobile telephones is also an option: ultimately, the greater the communications links, the closer the relationship will become.*

This is actually a question about communications technology, not about relationship marketing or about managing distribution channels, although it does provide scope for discussing all three. The focus should, however, be on the communications tools which might be used.

TASK FIVE

Explain, with examples, **TWO** benefits that marketing can bring to organisations **AND TWO** benefits it can bring to consumers.

(**4 marks**)

Specimen answer: *Good marketing will attract and retain customers and will also act as a coordinating force within the firm. For example, a good sales promotion such as a bring-a-friend scheme can bring in new customers, and a staff newsletter can convey the company's values and mission to staff, enabling them to coordinate their activities around customer satisfaction. Consumers benefit from marketing mainly because good marketing* *makes products available which meet customer needs more effectively than others. They also benefit by being given information about the products, both in terms of knowing about its features and benefits, and also about where the product can be bought.*

There are many other benefits of marketing for consumers and society at large – for example, advertising pays for a great many free services such as the Internet and television, and it subsidises transport, newspapers, magazines and even some public services such as schools and hospitals.

TASK SIX

Describe **TWO** ways in which the marketing department of a haulage company could respond to external pressures for the company to become more environmentally responsible.

(**4 marks**)

Specimen answer: *The marketing department should begin by consulting with the pressure groups to find out exactly what the problems are, especially asking whether the company is worse than others in the same industry. The company should respond to the problems as quickly as possible and should ensure that the solutions are well publicised through a PR campaign. For example, if the pressure group identifies pollution from the company's lorries as the major problem, the company should find ways to reduce exhaust emissions, or should consider replacing the fleet, perhaps over a period of years.*

The risk with this question is that the candidate gets sidetracked into 'theory dumping' everything he or she knows about societal marketing or corporate social responsibility. This is not required – this question is a straight application of the theory to a practical issue.

TASK SEVEN

Identify and explain **TWO** reasons why distribution channel analysis is an important part of the marketing audit.

(**4 marks**)

Specimen answer: *Distribution channels exist to get the product to the customer in the most efficient way possible. The first reason why the analysis is import is that it enables the company to decide whether the existing* *channel is close enough to the end consumer, in other words whether the Place element of the 7Ps is correct. The second reason for conducting a distribution channel analysis is concerned with logistics: are the products arriving in the best condition, via the most cost-effective transportation, taking account of all the factors? For example, a clothing importer might decide that a particular retail chain does not have the appropriate customer base for the products, or might decide that a particular wholesaler does not have the necessary fleets of lorries for moving the goods to the right retailers.*

On this type of question many candidates would try to write everything they know about the marketing audit, whereas the question is actually about distribution channel analysis, with examples of why the distribution channel is important.

TASK EIGHT

Identify **TWO** communications tools that could be used in the decline stage of the product life cycle.

(4 marks)

Specimen answer: *Reminder advertising could be used to bring the product back to people's attention, but if the product really is declining then a sales promotion could help it back up again. Reminder advertising is used to move a product back up the consumer's agenda by reminding them of its benefits. Sales promotion is usually used to create a short-term rise in sales, but in the case of a declining product it will help to re-establish the product on consumers' shelves: if there is a sales promotion aimed at the distribution channel this could also help.*

This question is about communications, not about the product life cycle. There is no need to discuss the PLC beyond the decline stage – the examiner will not give extra marks for it and it simply wastes your time.

TASK NINE

Identify and explain **TWO** suitable marketing communication media that could be used by a grocery retailer.

(4 marks)

Specimen answer: *A grocery retailer (e.g. Tesco's) is offering its products to a very wide range of people, so mass media would be most appropriate.*

Television is an obvious choice, because it reaches a very large number of people at a relatively low cost-per-thousand and it has the advantage that products can be shown and demonstrated. Despite the high headline cost, TV provides a powerful way to reach a large audience. Newspapers or other mass print media would also be suitable, since they are a permanent medium and coupons and special offers can be included, thus increasing the likely take-up of the offers.

This question is asking you about very specific circumstances. The communications media should be suitable for the purposes of a grocery retailer – another type of business might well require an entirely different set of media.

TASK TEN

Explain, with examples, the relationship between price and promotion.

(**4 marks**)

Specimen answer: *Price is more than just the amount of money the customer exchanges for the product. Price can signal quality (a high price is assumed to be associated with high-quality products), it can be used as a sales promotion (a reduction in price for a specified period will usually increase sales) and it can be used as a negotiating point by salespeople. Prices also help to position the brand against competing brands in people's minds: some products are perceived as being cheap, others as being expensive and there are many examples of this. One is the difference between Ford and BMW. The higher price of the BMW is associated with higher quality, greater prestige and a wealthier owner. Sales promotions for fast-moving consumer goods are often based on money-off, as are products offered in retailers' sales. Salespeople will often use a reduced price as a way of negotiating a larger order or a purchase of other products in the range.*

Again, this is very much an applied question. Simply writing out everything you know about pricing will not work.

(**Total 40 marks**)

SUMMARY

The short questions are mainly intended to test your knowledge, but you still will not be able simply to 'brain dump' the theory and hope to pass.

Many of the questions will test your understanding – Task 10 above does this – and your ability to think outside the box. Also, the questions will be taken from right across the syllabus, which means you will not be able to 'cherry-pick' and only revise part of the syllabus.

The reason for this is that Marketing Essentials is the foundation course for the rest of the Certificate, so it has to form a solid base from which you can go on to specialise. This does not mean that you have to know everything in order to pass – the pass mark is still 50% – but it does mean that you will have to have a broad range of knowledge to gain a high grade. Bearing in mind that you may make mistakes in the exam, you might misunderstand a question, you might simply be unable to make the necessary connections when you are working under pressure, you should insure yourself by studying every aspect to the best of your ability.

Try to answer every question, even if you are unsure of the right answer. Failure to attempt a question means you lose all 4 marks – even a bad answer might gain you a couple of marks and you might surprise yourself by remembering something you thought you had forgotten once you actually start writing.

Appendix Answers

CHAPTER 1

Case study answers

Tesco

1. Having low costs coupled with high prices must have made Tesco very profitable in the 1950s and the early 1960s. Why would Jack Cohen have lobbied for the abolition of Resale Price Maintenance? *Cohen saw that he had a clear competitive advantage, because his supermarkets had a lower cost base than traditional corner shops and therefore he could undercut other shops. Removing price controls would therefore benefit him in the long run – as indeed has proved to be the case. Providing customers with better value for money (which does not necessarily mean lowest possible prices, of course) is always advantageous.*

2. Presumably Tesco's various customer-focused innovations cost money. Why not simply cut prices even further? *Price is not the only way to compete. Most people do not buy the cheapest – they buy products which represent best value for money. Providing extras such as the 'one in front' policy creates a better value proposition, at relatively low cost to the firm – the value to the customer is vastly greater than would be the tiny reduction in prices the company could make if it did away with the policy.*

3. Why have three separate own-brand labels? *The separate own-brand labels exist to provide for the needs of different segments of the market. Price-sensitive customers use value brands: people seeking value for money look for the ordinary Tesco brand, and people seeking something luxurious might buy the Tesco's Finest. The Finest brand does not actually compete head-on with national brands in the way that the ordinary Tesco brand does.*

4. What is the difference between the trading-stamp system and the loyalty-card system? What advantages do loyalty cards have for customers and for Tesco's? *Loyalty cards have the major advantage that they enable Tesco to record individual customers' purchasing patterns. This allows Tesco's to plan better for meeting customer needs and also to target special offers and promotions more accurately. From the customer's viewpoint, the cards are much more convenient, and having special offers which are accurately targeted reduces the amount of junk mail the customer receives.*

5. Why stock a range of organic products as well as ordinary products? *Stocking organic products enables Tesco to meet the needs of a health-conscious group of people: at the same time, organic products tend to be more expensive, so the majority of Tesco's customers currently prefer the cheaper factory-farmed products.*

Legoland

1. What is Lego doing that most of its competitors are not doing? *Lego is appealing directly to its young customers by means of opening stores that are customer-friendly for children. It is also using parallel distribution: most toy manufacturers operate through retailers, but Lego also sells direct to the consumers.*

2. Lego's consumers are children, but the customers are the parents. How does Lego address this? *Because the children make their wishes known to their parents, Lego seeks to involve the parents in the process by means of the theme park. Parents bring their children to the park as a way of entertaining them and enjoying a day out, but they are then exposed to the educational and creative advantages of the toy.*

3. What is the coordinating role of Lego's approach? *Lego seeks to coordinate everything the firm does through the theme park idea. The franchising, production, licensing and distribution deals all rely on the fundamental view that children are individuals.*

4. How is Lego using its marketing philosophy to expand the business? *Lego extends the business via franchising and licensing deals, thus increasing the number of products which can be bought bearing the Lego brand. Considering the needs of its customers (the parents) and the consumers (the children) are the driving forces behind this approach.*

Bribery and Big Business

1. Why should not Lockheed continue to offer bribes in countries where this is normal business practice? *Lockheed should not offer bribes because it leads to a spiralling effect – the more companies offer bribes, the more they come to be expected. The company would be better occupied in seeking to stamp out bribery and compete on a level playing field.*

2. How might governments stop bribery from happening? *Governments do have the option of imposing large fines or imprisonment on people who accept bribes, but they can also impose sanctions on companies who offer them. An effective method is to allow people who accept bribes to keep the money provided they tell the authorities about the bribery.*

3. Is bribery an appropriate use of shareholders' money? *Bribery can be appropriate in the sense that shareholders' interests are best served by corporate growth: however, in the long term bribery will push up costs.*

4. Why is bribery damaging? *Bribery ultimately results in poorer quality firms prospering, with consequent damage to consumer interests. This is apart from the effects on the morals of the people giving and receiving bribes.*

União Digital Periféricos LTDA

1. Why are relationships so important for União Digital? *União Digital operates in a culture where personal relationships are important. The company also has to deal across very large distances: many of the firm's agents operate far from the company and may not therefore be as assiduous in looking after the company's interests as they might be were it not for the close relationships involved.*

2. Why would the company use the impersonal medium of a website to improve its relationships rather than spend more effort and money on personal contacts via salespeople? *Websites offer an excellent way to maintain contact over very long distances, at relatively low cost. Paying salespeople to cover the territory of South America would be prohibitively expensive: it could easily take more than a day's travel to visit a single customer.*

3. What role did BearingPoint's relationship marketing have in the process? *BearingPoint's own network of suppliers, and especially its close relationship with Cisco Systems, enabled the company to*

develop a complete system for União Digital. An essential element of developing networks is to have access to a wide range of firms.

4. How might União Digital further improve its relationship marketing? *União Digital might improve its relationships by continuing to consult its customers, by meeting with customers at every opportunity (e.g. at exhibitions and trade shows). The company should also consider customer win-back tactics.*

5. What are the specific advantages for União Digital in retaining customers? *União Digital would face exceptionally high costs in recruiting new customers due to geographical distances. Recruitment is likely to be largely undertaken by salespeople rather than by direct mail or other means: salespeople are expensive in such a widespread geographical area.*

Self-test answers

1. B Customer service is crucial in developing customer relationships.

2. A The other two are aspects of relationship marketing.

3. B The correct order is production, product, sales, marketing and societal.

4. B Production orientation and sales orientation have nothing to do with leadership styles: they are strategic positions.

5. A Setting common goals is necessary to coordination of departments.

CHAPTER 2

Case study answers

Sainsbury's

1. Why might Sainsbury's have revised the cost savings objective? *Sainsbury would do this in the light of having over-achieved. Objectives should always be subject to revision in the event of a change in circumstances – they should be a guide, not a straitjacket.*

2. How do the objectives relate to the vision statement? *The objectives come directly from the vision statement since the company seeks to increase overall revenue and profit (which will satisfy shareholder needs) by creating a better offer for customers. The objectives are all*

concerned with returning the Sainsbury brand to its former prominence.

3. How might Sainsbury's management have arrived at the stated objectives? *Partly, these objectives have arisen as a result of looking at the firm's competitive position and, partly, they have looked at their financial position. The objectives mainly arose, however, from the company's recovery plan and the MSGA vision.*

4. How realistic is the new Sainsbury's 3-year plan? *Given the recent gains the company has made, and the fact that they have exceeded the previous objectives, the new 3-year plan seems eminently achievable. In that sense, it is a good set of objectives: achieving the achievable is motivating for all concerned and reassuring for shareholders.*

Procter and gamble

1. What is the role of corporate culture in P&G's objective setting? *Corporate culture is key to the objective setting: P&G have to consider how their staff will respond to the changes and they are seeking to devolve a great deal of strategic decision making to local managers. This means that there is a real danger of the company having many different outcomes unless there is a string corporate culture binding staff together.*

2. Why did the Organisation 2005 initiative fail? *The main reason this initiative failed appears to be that it was too much change, too fast. The rapid shift in corporate culture upset some managers, who did not 'buy into' the changes, and consequently did not implement them successfully.*

3. What does the case study tell us about visionary leadership? *Visionary leaders can often be less than sensitive to staff needs: in pursuit of the vision, they may forget that their employees share a different vision.*

4. Why is P&G following a formal planning approach? *Formal planning enables the firm to ensure consultation with all interested parties, in an effort to ensure that most people will support the changes. In a corporation of this size, a degree of formal planning helps ensure some consistency across the range of activities being undertaken.*

5. How might P&G resolve the inevitable conflicts between GBUs and MDOs? *These conflicts can only be resolved by communication and negotiation between the parties at grass-roots level. Any attempt to*

impose decisions from senior management will only result in alienating the local managers and making them feel disempowered.

Amway

1. What were the objectives of DeVos and Van Andel in setting up Amway? *DeVos and Van Andel appear to have had an ethical or socially responsible driver for setting up Amway. The company was started on the basis of an ideal – the American Way of being self-sufficient and enterprising – and the founders not only believe in this themselves, but wanted to encourage other people to believe in it. Obviously, the new company needed to be profitable in order to survive – and the aim of growth is another strong element in Amway's objectives – but the main element is the founders' joint vision of a worldwide group of entrepreneurs creating an independent living for themselves.*

2. How are objectives communicated to the workforce? *The company communicates objectives in two main ways: first, its group leaders are sent on regular training courses at which company policies are promoted and the corporate culture is strengthened and, second, the IBOs are invited to regular 'pep talk'-type meetings at which enthusiasm for the Amway ethos is engendered. The company also communicates its strict code of ethical conduct in writing to IBOs and group leaders.*

3. How have technological influences affected Amway? *The main technological influence on Amway has been, of course, the Internet. This has made shopping from home extremely easy and convenient, which was of course Amway's main advantage over traditional retailers. Amway need to respond to this either by offering their products online (which would harm the interests of the IBOs) or by allowing IBOs to have their own websites (which might well dilute the brand values). Simply ignoring the Internet is not an option – the company's products would be forced into direct competition with other mainstream brands available through online retailers.*

4. What have been the cultural and social influences on Amway's business practices? *Cultural and social influences include the need for foreign cultures to buy into the 'American way' of entrepreneurship and independence – something which is alien to many cultures. For many people, there is an ethical problem in selling to friends and family, and there is of course a cultural problem in acting independently or (in some cases) of going into business at all. Amway*

has responded to some of these issues by demonstrating its credentials as a good corporate citizen – its strict code of practice, its community development programmes and its sponsorship of worthy events help to make people feel good about the company. This has helped to overcome the tarnished image of multi-level marketing.

5. How has legislation affected the firm? *Legislation has affected the firm seriously in many ways. The advent of pyramid schemes has caused governments to introduce legislation, but because each country has taken a different approach to tackling the problem, Amway has had to set up different systems in different countries, which creates major problems in terms of global corporate policy. Legislation concerning product formulation has been less of a problem, but still represents a potential threat, especially as environmental concerns become more important and governments might be expected to ban certain ingredients.*

Self-test answers

1. B is correct. The others are invented.

2. C is correct. Enlarging the market cannot be carried out by increasing profitability (although the reverse might be true) and likewise increasing profitability will not increase market share (again, the reverse might well be true).

3. B is correct. Aspirations of staff members and resource constraints are both part of the internal environment.

4. A is correct. Technological advances may come from competitors and may alter the resource constraints, but they are part of the external environment.

5. B is correct. The order is as follows:

   - Corporate objectives are set.

   - Marketing audit.

   - Setting business and marketing objectives.

   - Marketing strategies.

   - Marketing tactics/mix decisions.

   - Implementation.

   - Monitoring and control.

CHAPTER 3

Case study answers

HJ Heinz

1. Why might Heinz drop its pet foods range, when the products were still making money for the firm? *The pet foods range may have been making money, but since the range would require a completely separate marketing programme, it seems likely that resources would have been better directed towards new products in the food for humans range. There would undoubtedly be marketing synergies and economies of scale which would not exist in the pet food market. It is also possible that the pet food range was too small a part of an essentially stable, even stagnating market: as 'Dog' products, the pet food range might have been too unattractive to remain in the portfolio.*

2. What is the importance of packaging to Heinz? *Packaging enables Heinz to show a corporate image through the Keystone design and also provides possibilities for making the product more attractive, as with the turquoise colour of the baked beans can and the squeezable ketchup bottle. In common with other food companies, Heinz is required to provide nutritional information on the packaging, and can use the packaging to promote other products.*

3. How has the Heinz brand developed across the range? *The original 57 Varieties slogan and the keystone link the brand, but brand managers have been able to operate within this framework to develop individual images for products. The brands therefore reinforce each other, while retaining their individual personalities. This process could be developed further.*

4. What other changes might Heinz introduce to coordinate the branding better? *Heinz could coordinate the colour of its brands and could extend the 57 Varieties idea further. Establishing an overall Heinz brand personality would help: promoting the entire group of brands as one entity, carrying out cross-promotions in which one product is used as a promotional tool for others, and perhaps promoting the traditional values of the company would also help in establishing the firm's brand identity. This may require a shift in the corporate culture and systems, since each sub-brand apparently operates as an independent entity.*

5. Why might the company subdivide its brands into eight categories? *Categorising the products into branding groups makes it easier to*

*administer and control the marketing activities and also enables
Heinz to produce a more coherent and coordinated campaign within
each category. Dividing the overall range of 6,000 varieties enables
brand managers to build up expertise in specific markets (e.g. baby
foods require special marketing techniques, and seafood requires
special purchasing and packaging systems) and gives the company the
opportunity to establish itself as an expert in specific areas, rather
than a generalist food marketing company.*

Smith and Nephew

1. Why would Smith and Nephew sell off its consumer products
   divisions? *Smith and Nephew clearly decided that the ethical medical
   market (sales to medical professionals and hospitals) was more
   lucrative and less trouble than selling in consumer markets. The
   markets are bigger and require (in most cases) much less marketing
   expenditure. Also, in such a field as medicine companies need to
   show themselves as specialists rather than generalists – dealing with
   professional medical people is a skilled and delicate matter.*

2. Why does the company spend such a large portion of its turnover on
   research? *Medical science moves forward very quickly, and other
   firms in the supply side of the industry spend similar amounts on
   R&D. If Smith and Nephew fail to match this expenditure, they will
   be left (eventually) with an obsolete product line: product life cycles
   are short, in other words.*

3. What stage of the PLC was Band-Aid in during 1924? *Band Aid was in
   the introduction stage in 1924: it was almost certainly not yet a truly
   profitable line. At this point, relatively few people would know the
   product or be aware of its advantages, and the company would
   probably be spending a relatively large proportion of the marketing
   budget on trying to establish the product in its market.*

4. What stage of the PLC was Elastoplast in when Smith and Nephew
   sold it? *Elastoplast would be in the maturity stage, since there is still
   demand for the product but it is facing strong competition from cheap
   imitators. Essentially, it is currently stable, well known and requiring
   relatively low marketing expenditure to retain its market share. It is
   not yet in the decline phase, since there is nothing available to replace
   it apart from very similar 'me-too' products available from close
   competitors.*

5. To what extent are Smith and Nephew's products customer-specified?
Most of Smith and Nephew's products for professionals are customer-specified. The health care professionals need to be involved in identifying needs for new products, in all the fields in which the company operates: consultation with health professionals is essential. Even when the company develops new products, input from healthcare professionals is crucial.

Gillette

1. How did Gillette develop his original idea for a disposable razor blade?
Gillette began by noticing a need, then went through the development process of finding a technique for manufacturing the blades. Business analysis showed that he could not manufacture the blades cheaply enough without very large-scale production, so market testing demonstrated that giving the razors away would generate large enough sales of blades to make the project viable.

2. Why does the company innovate so much? *Many of Gillette's products can be easily copied by competitors, so developing new ones is a good way to keep ahead of the competition. Products quickly become obsolete as competitors enter, and for some products (batteries, etc.) technological change means rapid obsolescence. Few, if any, of Gillette's products can be protected effectively by patents.*

3. How does Gillette handle the problem of new products cannibalising sales of existing products? *Gillette is not unhappy about new products taking over sales of existing products, but the company sells existing products at lower prices and encourages consumers to 'trade up' to the new ones. Keeping obsolescent products in the range for as long as possible allows the company to harvest from its Dogs and Dodos, and also shuts out competitors effectively.*

4. What was the relationship between marketing and production in the case of the original blades? *In the original case, marketing drove production. Especially in the area of pricing, Gillette worked with the market: production would never have reached an economic level without his innovative approach. In fact, Gillette need never have manufactured anything – the whole of production could have been subcontracted.*

5. How might trading up work in global markets? *In a global market, obsolescent products can be re-launched in less developed markets, with the more up-to-date products following on later so that people*

can then trade up. This allows the company to obtain a maximum return on its development costs, while opening up new markets for the later products.

Innovations catalogue

1. How might Innovations seek to overcome the lack of a clear target market? *To an extent, the segmentation problem is self-correcting since people are able to search the catalogue by category. However, this implies that people are seeking products which apply to a specific hobby, interest or work situation, whereas people may well be just looking for 'wild and wacky' products, as gifts or as novelty items. Innovations could address this group by offering a 'weird' category, although inventors might be offended by this!*

2. What might be the appeal of Innovations to the average person? *Innovations makes interesting reading, but more importantly it offers newness in the products it markets. In some cases, the gadgets are directly useful; in other cases, they make interesting novelties or gifts. It may be that the products fulfil a 'hunter-gatherer' instinct in that visitors to the site might find something unexpected and will certainly find items that are interesting and stimulating.*

3. What factors have enabled Innovations to maintain its success? *A general interest in novelty on the part of consumers, the word-of-mouth potential of the products and the accessibility of its website (and the previous catalogue) are the main contributors. The products themselves often have entertainment value – they are interesting or humorous, and consequently the catalogue is worth reading. Finally, Innovations has been prepared to embrace new technology by moving itself to the Internet.*

4. Why would somebody buy fun-fur-lined golf club covers? *This is clearly a fun, novelty item: it is the type of product which is bought for 'the man who has everything' or by someone wanting to distinguish his or her golf clubs from everyone else's. The likelihood is that the product will be bought as a gift rather than for personal use, in other words – something which probably applies to a great many of Innovations' products.*

The international software market

1. What is the role of consumer characteristics in software price setting? *Consumers may want very different things from the software and*

have very different ideas on what is worth paying for and what is not. In different parts of the world, wealth and price perceptions clearly play a role: what appears cheap in one market appears expensive in another, and people's view of what represents value for money will also vary according to the cost of other products in the market, especially those against which people make comparisons.

2. Why should companies not charge one price for everyone, regardless of location? *Perceptions of value for money will differ greatly between wealthy countries and poorer countries, since people are likely to translate prices in terms of how many hours they need to work to buy the item. Charging a lower price in poorer countries is still economically viable for software companies, since the upfront costs of developing the software have been met by consumers in wealthy countries. Charging a lower price simply opens up extra revenue at little cost.*

3. Why might the product not represent the same value for money in each of its markets? *Value for money is based on what the product will do for the customer. In a wealthy market, the labour savings gained by using computers soon pay for the software, because labour is expensive: in poorer countries the gains are less obvious, since pay is much lower. Software costing £100 represents a day's pay to the average Briton, but perhaps 3 months' earnings to the average Indian. Of course, wealth concentration is higher in India, so the 'average' Indian is unlikely to be in the market for either a computer or the software to run on it.*

4. The market is huge, so why is there not room for many players to compete? *Because of standardisation and compatibility issues, one standard for the world is likely to emerge. Competition is therefore aimed at dominating the entire market, not just at capturing a section of it: in a sense, there is only one market to go for. Smaller players have very little chance of entering the market, because of the economies of scale involved: the huge upfront costs of developing software can only be amortised over a very large production run, hence the product orientation is commonly seen in the software market.*

5. How might a new software supplier (e.g. an Indian or Chinese supplier) price its products effectively in the world market? *New suppliers would probably enter the market competing on price at first, but (given that their products would have to be compatible with other products) an Indian of Chinese supplier would still need to enter the*

world market on a similar pricing structure as the current major players, since they would find it difficult or impossible to fight a lengthy price war.

Internet auctions

1. How might a manufacturer retain a skimming policy when dealing with a reverse auction? *Manufacturers can set a series of price levels according to the quantities bought and can set those levels wherever they want: this is, in effect, what skimming does. However, there is no control over when each price applies, only over the number of people needed to trigger the next price reduction. This means that people who would have been prepared to pay a higher price will in fact obtain the product at the lower price, which destroys the point of skimming.*

2. How might a car dealer encourage a prospective customer to increase the tender price? *Car dealers can offer extras, but in particular a car dealer might be able to offer something which other car dealers are unable or unlikely to match, for example, free delivery to the customer's home or free driving lessons for the customer's older children.*

3. What advantages might there be for manufacturers in participating in reverse auctions? *From a manufacturer's viewpoint, a reverse auction represents an opportunity to sell a lot of products in one sale, often for more than would be the case if the firm went through wholesalers. However, the extra administrative effort and the possibility of annoying the existing distributors might outweigh the benefits. Clearly, it is in the manufacturer's interests to sell large quantities of product in one hit, but not at the expense of damaging the existing distribution chain, which will undoubtedly represent the bulk of the business.*

4. How might a manufacturer calculate the appropriate price bands for a reverse auction? *Manufacturers would need to take account of the economies of scale involved in making a bulk sale, the extra administrative burden of dealing with the sales, and the extra risks involved. They would also need to consider delivery costs to a lot of individuals rather than to a single distributor, and the potential costs attached to auctions which fail to reach the minimum number needed to make the sale worthwhile.*

5. What might retailers do to counteract the effects of reverse auctions? *Retailers probably have little to fear from reverse auctions, as they are time-consuming and potentially unproductive for consumers – the savings may well be outweighed by the hassles. Having said that, retailers should be able to emphasise the greater convenience, the availability of advice and the quality of their after-sales service. Retailers can generally compete well, provided they offer a good enough service to their customers – which is, of course, the basis of marketing.*

C.A. Papaellina & Co. Ltd.

1. What advantages does Novartis gain from dealing through CAP? *Novartis gains comprehensive distribution throughout Cyprus, even to small street-corner kiosks. Pharmaceutical distribution needs to be very responsive, due to the short shelf life of some medicines and the fact that pharmacies do not stock everything. This means that Novartis needs a firm which can respond rapidly to any delivery requirements.*

2. Why might CAP have bought into retail outlets? *CAP has bought into retailers as a means of creating vertical integration. This will streamline the distribution and remove the problem of controlling (or being controlled by) other members of the distribution chain. Retaining this level of control could be important to CAP in such a small overall market, especially as European Union membership has increased the possibility of other firms entering the Cypriot market.*

3. What specific problems might a confectionery manufacturer have when approaching the Cypriot market? How might CAP be able to help? *Confectionery is affected by heat, and Cyprus is a hot place, so delivery will need to be expeditiously carried out. Also, confectionery is sold largely through kiosks, which means having the capability to deliver very small amounts to places which are often hard to access using large delivery vehicles. CAP can help because it has a comprehensive delivery system which operates daily deliveries to retail outlets throughout the island.*

4. What are the major differences between supplying hypermarkets and supplying kiosks? *Hypermarkets will accept very large deliveries at a time: large lorries can be used, whereas a kiosk will require deliveries in small amounts, possibly by handcart. Also, invoicing for a hypermarket can be done by each individual manufacturer if*

necessary – such an approach would be hopelessly uneconomic when dealing with kiosks, so an intermediary is essential.

5. Why would competing manufacturers such as Chanel and Jean Paul Gaultier be prepared to use the same distributor? *Although these manufacturers are competing, they do need distribution to the same outlets. In Cyprus, there is relatively little choice about who distributes to the target retailers: CAP is probably the only choice. Ensuring that one's products are offered from the same outlets as competing products is actually essential if people are to be able to make comparisons: such comparisons should result in increased business, unless of course the competitor's product is better.*

Giant bicycles

1. What are the advantages of using a firm like Wincanton? *Wincanton supply specialist services and are already familiar with distribution in most or all of Giant's markets overseas. Wincanton can also operate more efficiently when delivering to small outlets, since they would be able to fill a truck or container with goods bound for nearby destinations.*

2. How might Giant Bicycles enter markets where Wincanton are not represented? *Giant might look for a local distributor or agent, or might operate through wholesalers in the area. It may be possible for them to find another logistics firm able to fill the gaps in Wincanton's coverage.*

3. What are the main problems Giant faces in terms of logistics? *The main problems are the global nature of the business, the differing sizes of retail outlets, the location of outlets in terms of national transportation infrastructure and (occasionally) the small delivery quantities.*

4. What challenges Wincanton face in the 21st century? *Wincanton are facing problems from global competition and from the rapid growth in alternative distribution systems. A growing expectation for just-in-time delivery, and an impatience with failed deliveries, will also impact the firm. Increased customer expectations, particularly regarding delivery reliability and order tracking, may also affect Wincanton's operations.*

5. What type of information might the companies exchange via their mutual IT systems? *The main type of information will be order tracking, since customers will contact Giant with the query but Giant*

may not have the information. Sales forecasts would be useful for Wincanton to have, since these will help with their own forward planning, and obviously ordering information will be important.

Scotiabank

1. How did Scotiabank translate its vision statement into an advertising campaign? *The vision statement was about treating people as individuals and finding solutions which would help make them wealthy – a very customer-orientated vision. The bank used this to develop a campaign showing people in typical 'problem' situations, then showing how the bank could help solve the problem.*

2. What sales promotion techniques did Scotiabank use? *The bank used the cash back mortgage, the business and personal banking facility, and a hand-holding approach to online banking. These sales promotions encouraged loyalty, but they also encouraged people towards dependency on the bank for sorting out all sorts of financial problems.*

3. How did the three principles translate into an integrated communications campaign? *By using the problem–solution format, Scotiabank was able to show typical, relevant problems and show the solution (thus meeting the focus on the truth of people's lives principle). The bank showed how it could help people to generate wealth for themselves (the getting ahead principle) and by understanding how people were usually treated by other banks they were able to see things from the customer's perspective.*

4. What difficulties might there have been in offering a single, integrated message to such a wide range of potential customers? *The main problem would be ensuring that people felt that the message was relevant to them. Seeing people in typical problem situations would certainly have helped to convey the message: most of the situations would be fairly stereotypical of people's involvement with banks.*

Viral marketing

1. Advertising is heavily regulated: it must, by and large, be truthful. No such regulations exist on contacts between friends, so why is viral marketing more credible than advertising? *Credibility is about the source, not about the regulations surrounding it. People are more likely to trust someone they know, especially if the person has no obvious vested interest, rather than a stranger with an obvious*

interest in making the sale. Interpersonal communications will always be more credible than impersonal ones because the individuals concerned can read each others' facial expressions and body language more easily.

2. How might the power of word of mouth be transferred to advertising? *Some advertising models word of mouth by showing friends advising each other: this is a common ploy in household products advertising. Another approach is to encourage people to tell a friend by offering incentives, either to the adviser or to the friend or to both. In general, giving a reward to the friends works better than giving a reward to the existing customer.*

3. What type of organisation might benefit most from viral marketing on the Internet? *Any organisation which is offering goods which are useful to computer owners and users, and any organisation aiming for a younger market would benefit from Internet-based viral marketing. On a more subtle level, any organisation which has difficulty in identifying the members of its target market would gain from viral marketing, because people tend to become friends with people much like themselves and will therefore tend to send them items they find interesting.*

4. What other advertising media might be useful in driving customers to the website? *Almost any other medium can be used to drive customers to the website: firms often use billboard or press advertising to do so, and even TV can be used. Recently, firms have been using e-mail viruses to drive potential customers to websites, but this is widely regarded as unethical. Probably print is most suitable because the URL can be printed – broadcast media such as TV and radio are impermanent, and it is unlikely that someone watching a TV ad would be quick enough or alert enough to write down a web address.*

Full stop

1. What are the main communication factors which would prevent the NSPCC reaching its goal? *One major problem the NSPCC has is that child abuse is a distressing topic: many people are likely to shy away from overly-emotional portrayals of abuse victims, and thus the impact of the advertising will be lost. On the other hand, the issue has to be confronted in a realistic way. A further factor is the difficulty of conveying complex information about how to recognise and report child abuse, when the advertisements are only a few seconds long.*

2. How might the NSPCC be more proactive in contacting potential abusers? *The NSPCC could run a hotline for parents who feel unable to cope and could also liaise closely with the police and other agencies to work with parents who are or who might become abusers. Although currently much of this work is carried out by local authority Social Services departments, the NSPCC could also contribute.*

3. What other communications media might the NSPCC use? *Most media are already used by the charity, including TV, radio, direct mail, press, outdoor media and Internet-based media. The charity should look at viral campaigns, thus approaching a younger audience who are comfortable with 'word of mouse' communications.*

4. What are the main problems for the NSPCC in producing an integrated campaign? *The NSPCC has a major problem in that it is trying to communicate to a wide range of audiences, each of whom need a different message and each of whom will interpret messages intended for others. For example, a message intended to help abusive parents control themselves better may be construed as sympathetic to the abuser by some other observers. Also, the charity uses a wide range of media, each of which will offer a different type of media experience for the audience.*

5. How might the NSPCC improve the integration of its campaign? *Although it is difficult to integrate the campaign fully, some progress might be made by ensuring that the charity's main aim is always prominent. In this case, the NSPCC needs to ensure that its Full Stop strapline is used in all the communications, and to retain a common theme in the advertising. Integration would be easier if fewer media were used, but this would undoubtedly reduce the coverage the campaign receives.*

JD Wetherspoon

1. What is the role of physical evidence in Martin's thinking? *Physical evidence is exemplified in Wetherspoon's by the unique environment. There is no loud music, no TV and no noisy pub games, so customers have a relaxing and quiet atmosphere in which to enjoy their evening out.*

2. Why would Wetherspoon seek to have smoking banned in all pubs? *Banning smoking in pubs has been advantageous to Wetherspoon's because of their belief that many people avoid pubs because of the smoky atmosphere. Smokers are now a minority of the UK*

population, and smoking is becoming socially unacceptable: Wetherspoon's brand image (comfort, safety and clean surroundings) does not fit well with allowing smoking. Although many pubs appear to have lost business due to the ban, Wetherspoon's remains relatively buoyant.

3. Why ban music in the pubs? *Wetherspoon's emphasis on the physical evidence aspect of the service mix means that they are aiming for customers who seek out a quiet environment. Music detracts from this.*

4. Why might Wetherspoon's seek to limit people's drinking? *An important element in the People factor in the marketing mix is the other customers. Customers who become drunk might also become noisy, or even abusive and violent. This would harm the Wetherspoon's image: it is not worth damaging the brand simply for the short-term gain of selling a little more alcohol.*

Wetherspoon Lodges are a brand extension of the basic Wetherspoon's brand. It carries the same brand values as the Wetherspoon pub brand, but offers different benefits.

Insight express

1. How might Insight Express be able to help with assessing advertising effectiveness? *Measuring advertising effectiveness is notoriously difficult, because there are too many other variables that can account for any observed effects. Measuring communications effectiveness involves measuring communications outcomes rather than marketing outcomes, so Insight Express should be looking for such outcomes as brand awareness, corporate image or position of the brand with respect to competitors.*

2. What type of product would be reliably researched by Insight Express, and which would not? *Anything which involves computing would be an obvious target for Insight Express, since the respondents would obviously own (or at least regularly use) computers. Products which require physical inspection, for example, prototypes of new products, would probably not be suitable. Also, products which are aimed at low-income groups or older age groups might be difficult to research because of the demographic profile of Insight Express's typical respondents.*

3. Apart from sampling, what other problems might arise for Insight Express clients? *Because the respondents are self-selecting, they are*

likely to be people who will have strong opinions, or have a particular viewpoint they wish to express, or (in some cases) may have a malicious motive for joining the panel. Some people even join such panels for the rewards which they are sometimes offered. In any event, they are likely to differ somewhat from a randomly chosen sample of the population.

4. What factors might have biased the DVR research? *Levels of computer literacy and involvement, the degree to which people are prepared to answer questions honestly (in particular issues such as age and income which would not be apparent when the respondent is not physically present), and the degree to which it is possible to be dishonest when the researcher is not present are all rich sources of bias.*

5. What problems might arise from using the panel approach? *Because the same respondents are used each time, the panel members become used to the kind of questions which are asked and will often start thinking of themselves as 'expert witnesses' whose opinions are more important than other people's. This can be fatal for the conduct of research because the panel members begin to give an 'official' opinion instead of their own honest viewpoint.*

Manchester united football club

1. Which elements of the marketing mix does Manchester United use, and in what ways? *MUFC uses promotion via its website, TV channel and magazine. The company uses premium pricing for its products (the merchandise range) and also for its gate – watching MUFC play live is an expensive proposition. The actual product – entertaining football – is used as a device for merchandising. The place where the exchange takes place might be at the ground, over the Internet, or on TV: the matches might be seen or the merchandise purchased in several locations. The people element is mainly about the players, who deliver the service but (in this case) have virtually no contact with the consumers. Players have typically generated extensive PR coverage by being themselves newsworthy. The process of doing business is based around the football calendar and the scheduling of matches: the physical evidence is the merchandise itself.*

2. What type of pricing strategy might be most appropriate for MUFC? *MUFC use a premium pricing strategy, but might possibly use skimming when new strip comes on the market. In practice, since there is no possibility of competitors producing similar products (other*

teams' strips would not be acceptable to MUFC fans, and the club has copyright on its strip), there would be no need to reduce prices to meet competition.

3. What effect would your choice of pricing strategy have on the MUFC brand? *Premium pricing has the effect of enhancing the value of the brand, since price is a surrogate for quality. Skimming would be less effective.*

4. Which promotional devices would be most appropriate for MUFC? *Having their own TV channel clearly marks MUFC out as something very different, but as a global brand the emphasis needs to be on global media such as the Internet.*

5. Why might MUFC have such a large following outside the UK? *MUFC has been extremely successful on the pitch, especially in international contests, which means that TV coverage of MUFC matches has been both extensive and international. Global TV channels such as Sky have been instrumental in promoting MUFC since the quality of the play guarantees large audiences. The club has capitalised on this by using its own global media to enhance its position on the world stage.*

Self-test answers

1. What does PLC stand for? B *is the correct answer. The others are invented.*

2. Which of the following is true? C *is correct. The order is: idea generation, screening, concept testing, business analysis, product development, market testing and commercialisation.*

3. Which of the following is true? A *is true. For a retailer, product is the service element the retailer adds, not the products on the shelves, and price affects all the other elements of the mix.*

4. A new product which changes people's lives radically is called: B *is correct. Continuous innovation is merely a minor adjustment, and discontinuous innovation is still recognisable as its predecessor, whereas discontinuous innovation is truly new to the world.*

5. Which of the following is true? A *is correct. The order is: innovators, early adopters, early majority, late majority and laggards.*

6. Which of the following lists the elements of the traditional promotional mix? B *is correct. Price is part of marketing mix, and personal communication is usually regarded as being part of PR.*

7. Pitching the price low to start with in order to gain market share is called: A *is correct. Skimming means pricing high to start with, and demand pricing is about setting the price at a point which controls demand.*

8. Pitching the price high to start with then reducing it as competitors enter the market is called: A *is correct. Penetration pricing means pitching the price low to gain market share, and competitive pricing means pricing according to what competitors are charging.*

9. A firm which sells books on the Internet is an example of: C *is correct. Any firm which sells to final consumers is a retailer.*

10. The practice of moving goods through the distribution chain from raw materials to end user is called: B *is correct. Logistics is the science of supply – it includes physical distribution and is included in marketing.*

Index

179